A Short Introduction to Afro-American History

From Slavery to Freedom

(The untold story of Colonialism, Human Rights, Systemic Racism and Black Lives Matter – Student Edition)

Scholar Library Press

Disclaimer

From top left to bottom left:

Frederick Douglass (abolitionist), Sojourner Truth (activist), Martin Luther King Jr. (Activist), George Washington Carver (scientist)

Our other books

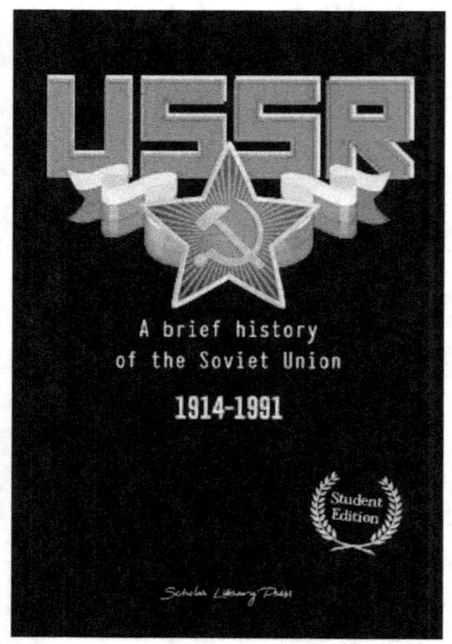

Interested in the history of the USSR?

The History of the USSR 1914-1991 is a comprehensive and authoritative account of one of the most important periods in modern world history. It traces events from Tsarist Russia, through to Lenin's Bolshevik Revolution, Stalin's rule, Khrushchev's "Thaw" and Brezhnev's stagnation - up to Gorbachev and beyond. This book offers an unrivalled perspective on Soviet society at every level - political, economic, social and cultural.

This book is a comprehensive account of the rise and fall of communism in Russia. The author examines how these leaders dealt with economic problems such as food shortages and unemployment. He also explores their foreign policies during World War II and afterward, when they tried to maintain an empire that was slipping out of their grasp.

You'll find out how people lived under communism; what they ate; where they went for entertainment; how their clothes were made; who was allowed to travel abroad or buy foreign goods; what happened when they fell ill or died. And you'll learn about all those things that are now so familiar, but which had not yet been invented then – mobile phones, computers, western movies... All these things have come into being since 1991 but this book will tell you what life was like before them.

You will be able to understand why this country fell apart so quickly after its inception by reading this book! There are plenty of lessons learned for those who want to study communist countries or just learn more about Russian history!

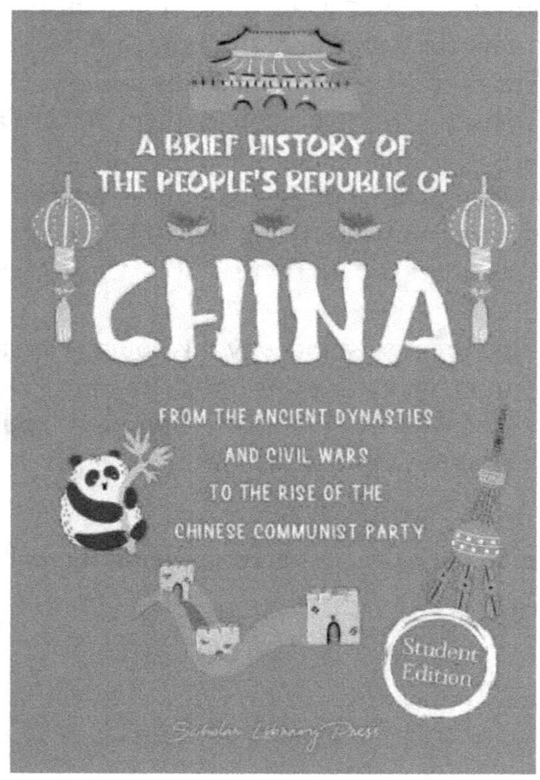

If you are interested in the history of China, this is a great book for you!

This book is a brief history of the People's Republic of China. It covers everything from Ancient Dynasties and Civil Wars to the Rise of the Chinese Communist Party. You can read about how it all started, what happened during Mao Zedong's rule, and more!

In 1949, the Chinese Communist Party (CCP) won its first victory and established the People's Republic of China. The CCP was led by Mao Zedong and his comrades-in-arms such as Zhou Enlai, Zhu De, Chen Yun and Deng Xiaoping. They led the people to fight against Japanese invaders and their domestic enemies including landlords, rich peasants, counterrevolutionaries, and bad elements who were sabotaging national reconstruction.

If you're interested in learning about this country's past, then this is a great place to start. The author has created an informative book that will give you a better understanding on what took place over time. It also includes pictures for visual learners who want to see images as well as words.

This book will tell you about how these leaders helped shape modern day China with their leadership skills that are still used today! You will learn about how they fought for equality among all classes in society while also building up an economy that could compete on a global scale. It is not just a story about politics or economics - it's also one of culture! Learn more about traditional customs from this brief history of China!

You can find this book in a paperback version on all major book store websites

Introduction

In this book we are going to talk about the history of African Americans, also called African Americans or Black Americans, these people are an ethnic group in the United States. Members are residents of the United States with full or partial African ancestry.

In 2000, there were 34.6 million African Americans in the United States; this is 12.3% of the U.S. population. They are overwhelmingly descendants of slaves brought to the U.S., but after the abolition of slavery in 1863, there has also been immigration from the Caribbean and from Africa itself; the result of this latter immigration flow is a population of about 800 000.

This population group has an educational history is denouncing many aspects of difficult pain points in contemporary society. It is extremely important to educate yourself on the history of slavery, colonialism and racism, and how it developed through the events and time frames described in this book.

How the name of this population group came about in history

Before we go into detail about each part, we will first briefly discuss how the name of this population group came about. During the period of slavery, until 1865, slaves of African descent were referred to as blacks or negroes. After the abolition of slavery, colored was introduced as an alternative, since both earlier designations recalled the painful past; however, Negroes, now capitalized, was also used by this group as a self-designation (e.g., still in Martin Luther King's speech I have a dream, 1963). The civil rights movement, however, also introduced the term African Americans, in order to strengthen its ties to its own origins, while Malcolm X and the Black Power movement reintroduced the ultimately more popular name blacks. The designation as African Americans stemmed from a proposal by Jesse Jackson, who wanted to replace categorization based on skin color with a more culturally charged designation.

A brief introduction to the timeline of history that we will cover in this book

The most important part of Afro-American history lies in the start of the slave trade in the United States, but prior to this topic, there was already the Trans-Atlantic slave trade that took place between 1525 and 1867, of which it is important to also include this part of history to paint a picture of what preceded the slave trade in what is now the United States.

At that time, the United States was a colony of several countries, mainly from Western Europe. it was also divided up differently, since there were no land borders as yet. It was also divided up differently, as there were no land borders to speak of today.

1700-1900

During the 18th and early 19th centuries, slaves were transported en masse from West Africa to the south of what is now the United States to be used as labor on the plantations there. They often died in inhumane conditions on the trip to America (famous is the rebellion on the Amistad in 1839 in the waters around Cuba, in which about forty African slaves rebelled and demanded the return trip to Africa, but were transported to America, sparking a heated debate that ended with their return to Africa). The slave trade was abolished in 1808, but this was not enough for people in the North, who wanted slavery as an institution to be abolished altogether. There were many movements working for this.

In 1860, Abraham Lincoln was elected president of the United States. Southerners were opposed to this president, partly because they were afraid he would end slavery. Therefore, the South declared its independence and was henceforth known as the Confederacy. Despite initial successes, the South eventually lost and was forced to release the slaves. In the South, some still deny that the American Civil War was about abolishing slavery; they believe it was about defending the autonomy of the states against federal authority. Many ex-slaves migrated to the North, where, incidentally, conditions were not much better because of racial hatred. Still, African Americans are by far the most concentrated in the territory of the former Confederacy.

1900-1970

The abolition of slavery did not make African-Americans equal; a system was put in place to keep whites and blacks separate in society, called segregation. This meant that blacks had to use different, often inferior, services than whites. In the 1950s, President Dwight D. Eisenhower reluctantly tried to end this. For example, forced by the Supreme Court, he opened several white schools in the South to blacks, leading to race riots.

A key figure for African Americans was Martin Luther King, a leader of the black civil rights movement. He led the march to Washington D.C. on August 28, 1963, where he gave his famous I Have a Dream speech. In 1964 he was awarded the Nobel Peace Prize. In 1968, he was shot dead by James Earl Ray. In 1983, the third Monday in January became a national holiday called Martin Luther King Day.

1970-2021

Black Americans are the only group that has been systematically discriminated against by the government and, if anything, given nothing. Until 1965, black residents of the U.S. were not free - that's when racial segregation was only removed from the statute books. Even though most people in America are no longer as openly racist as they were back then, racism is ingrained in the history of the United Statem. If we don't take a turn to correct that it will continue to affect how prosperous people become, and how black people are treated by the police right now.

The U.S. is built on racism. And some people want to defend that. They are preventing black people from exercising their fundamental rights. At the beginning of this year, armed white people in Michigan occupied a government building in protest. Imagine if a group of black people had done that! Then the situation could have ended in a terrible way.

Thanks to the civil rights movement of the 1960s, there was legislation that helped advance the bottom of society. But in the 1980s, President Ronald Reagan began cutting into that. As industry collapsed, so did jobs from neighborhoods to which many black Americans were condemned. Economic uncertainty followed, on top of that came an inordinately large police force that fought the war on drugs much more in black neighborhoods than in white ones.

Heavy prison sentences for minor drug offenses made prison a part of life in black communities. One in three black men spend time in prison, compared to only one in seventeen white men. All of those men continue to struggle for the rest of their lives to find a job, get government support, or even vote - which is no longer allowed in many states with a criminal record.

The criminal justice system is a new way of turning black people into second-class citizens, writer and lawyer Michelle Alexander showed in her classic The New Jim Crow. The progress that activists led by Martin Luther King managed to make in the 1960s has been undone by mass incarceration. In this book, we also address current events with African-American history as background and underpinning.

We hope the book is an educational experience that will enrich your perspective regarding this crucial part of world history. We also hope to contribute to the social importance of a fair society. our vision is that this can only be improved through education and transparency. Only by learning how your fellow man experiences his life can you consciously contribute positively to a better future.

If you like this book please leave a review to ensure that more people read it and we can spread a little awareness!

Table of Contents

Part 1: African heritage and the Trans-Atlantic slave trade

Chapter 1: Pre-colonial Africa

For most people who delve into this subject, the history of Africa begins from the 17th century (1600 A.D), when the then European powers carried out the first Trans-Atlantic slave shipments.

Just to briefly discuss a large time frame, between 200 000 and 100 000 years ago, modern humans began to evolve throughout Africa - including South Africa. They became the San, who later met the southward migrating Khoi nomads from the north, and they became collectively known as the Khoisan.

The Khoisan entered the Western Cape at about the same time (300 AD) that groups of the early Iron Age crossed the Limpopo, whose descendants, about 1 000 years later, formed the African Kingdom of Mapungubwe and established trade relations with China, India, and Arabia.

Egypt had early contacts deep into the hinterland of Africa. For example, Kush was a part of Egypt and regular expeditions left for the Horn of Africa, to Poent. During Egypt's unstable third interregnum, the Kushites began to break away from Egyptian pharaohs and established the autonomous state of Kush, with the cities of Napata (at the foot of the sacred mountain Djebel Barkal) and Meroe as the main centers of power. Kushite culture was strongly influenced by Egyptian culture. Thus, pyramids were also built here. However, these tombs were only about ten meters high and much steeper than the Egyptian pyramids.

Piye, king of Kush (Nubia) conquered all of Egypt around 740 BCE and founded Egypt's 25th dynasty, the period of the black pharaohs. With the help of the Assyrians, Psammetichus I was able to reconquer Egypt. He gained control of entire country in 656 BC .

According to tradition, the kingdom of Ethiopia was founded in 980 BC by Menelik I, the son of Solomon and the Queen of Sheba.

The ancestors of the Bantu peoples are thought to have begun to penetrate the Central African rainforest around 1000 BCE, probably along the major rivers. From there they would have reached the vicinity of Lake Victoria, which would become a secondary center from which they would spread across much of East Africa in the first centuries of our era.

Around the beginning of the era, the entire northern coast of Africa was part of the Roman Empire. This is also how the continent got its name: Africa was the Latin name for the region of land around present-day Tunisia. North Africa was one of the leading areas in terms of culture.

With the advent of Christianity, this entire area initially became Christian. Although the closing of the Isis temple in Elefantine was not welcomed by its southern neighbors, the new faith soon penetrated Nubia as well. Later it would spread to Ethiopia as well. With the advent of Islam, Nubia continued to adhere to the Coptic faith for a long time (until the 16th century), and the same is true of Ethiopia to this day.

In the fifth and sixth centuries, the great Ghanaian empire and Kanem-Bornu emerged in West Africa, invaded by its northern neighbors in the eleventh century. In 1230, the capital of Ghana fell. From the thirteenth to the mid-sixteenth century, the great Islamic empires of Songhai and Mali (capital Timbuktu) arose thereafter south of the Sahara. Mecca was built in large part from money from these flourishing kingdoms. During the same period, the Iron Age culture of Greater Zimbabwe flourished in southern Africa. This culture, according to artifacts found in the forts, had trade relations with China and others.

In contrast to the Mediterranean countries, slavery was virtually absent from the Republic of the Netherlands, England and France in the Late Middle Ages and Early Modern Era. It was unthinkable in this period that large groups of slaves would be sold in Amsterdam, London, or Nantes, as did happen in Lisbon and Cadiz. But although freedom was an important concept in the Republic and the abuse of the Indians was used as propaganda by the Spanish, the Dutch, as well as the English and French, saw no problem in trading slaves outside of Europe and using them on plantations.

In the Roman Republic and with the Greeks, anyone could fall prey to slavery, which was seen as a matter of misfortune. Under the influence of Christianity, slavery initially disappeared in Western Europe. The slave trade was considered immoral and went against Christian values.

This changed with the Trans-Atlantic slave trade. Here, justification was sought in the Bible, among other places, where in Genesis 9 the descendants of Cham - Martin Luther argued that Cham was the progenitor of all colored people - are cursed into slavery. The form of moral disconnection later changed by portraying the victims as inferior and barbaric, thus contributing significantly to the development of racism.

The fifteenth century

The rounding of Cape Bojador in 1434 by the Portuguese can be considered the beginning of the European voyages of discovery. In 1441 Antão Gonçalves bought the first black African slave and the following year he bought ten more. They were called "azenegue." In 1445, Nuno Tristão founded the first factory, Feitorias, on the island of Arguin. By the death of Henry, the Navigator in 1460, they had explored the West African coast as far as Cape Palmas, the beginning of the Gulf of Guinea.

In 1469, King Alfons V of Portugal granted the monopoly of the Gulf of Guinea to Fernão Gomes, a merchant from Lisbon, at an annual rent of 200,000 réis. The contract further stipulated that Gomes should continue the discoveries and sail up to one hundred leagues (150 miles) along the coast. During this period, the gold mines of Elmina were discovered, this became a driving force for further searches.

During the reign of King Johan II of Portugal (1481-1495), Diogo Cao discovered the mouth of the Congo River and rounded Bartolomeu Dias, Cape of Good Hope. During this period, the islands of Sao Tome and Principe were populated.

Vasco da Gama was the first European to sail around Africa (1497-1498). During the historic voyage in 1500 under Pedro Álvares Cabral, not only Brazil was discovered, but also Madagascar.

This century also marks the beginning of the Trans-Atlantic slave trade. Although the slave trade was already present in Africa, and for centuries there had been forced labor sold to surrounding countries, especially in the middle east. Was this the era when Europe colonized large parts of Africa on short notice for cheap labor and stealing resources.

This part of history about the details of the Trans-Atlantic slave trade will be further discussed in the next chapter.

Chapter 2: An overview of the Trans-Atlantic slave trade

The Trans-Atlantic slave trade was the trade in slaves from Africa to the Americas, conducted by Europeans. It was the middle passage of the triangular trade and took place between 1525 and 1867, peaking in the eighteenth century and the first half of the nineteenth century. An estimated 12 million slaves were transported.

The Trans-Atlantic slave trade was the trade in slaves from Africa to the Americas, conducted by Europeans. It was the middle passage of the triangular trade and took place between 1525 and 1867, peaking in the eighteenth century and the first half of the nineteenth century. An estimated 12 million slaves were transported.

The Trans-Atlantic slave trade brought mostly black Africans to North and South America. In Africa, the slaves were offered by local black leaders who, among other things, enslaved them in various wars. Instead of making these slaves work themselves to death, ceremonially killing them, or selling them to Arab traders as before, it proved more lucrative to sell them to the Europeans.

Thus, from Elmina in Ghana, 2,000 slaves per year were shipped to the Americas. There they were employed on plantations. Although slave trading in Africa existed before the Europeans intervened in it, the scale on which it took place thereafter was considerably larger. While the earlier numbers were not inconsiderable, the demographic impact was limited, and societies did not change significantly.

This changed with the Atlantic slave trade. Politically, the influence was also great. It triggered a militarization of African societies that led to state formation in which aggressive states such as Ashanti and Dahomey were at an advantage, while peoples such as the Yoruba, Benin, and the Mossi eventually went into decline. Economically it stimulated short-term solutions, while socially it led to division, where it is known to this day which ancestors were slave hunters.

A short history of Ashanti

In 1482, the Portuguese built the fortress of Elmina on the coast, originally because of gold mining there. This was the beginning of colonial contacts, which at first mainly involved the gold trade. Ghana Osei Tutu ruled between 1680 and 1717. Since the capture of the fortress of Elmina from the Portuguese in 1637, the Dutch traders of the West India Company were an important trading partner of the Ashanti, who supplied slaves for the triangular trade. In return, the Ashanti were given access to firearms, and this led to a tightening of internal political and social relations. By 1740, this trade had displaced the trade in gold and ivory from the first place

A short history of Dahomey

The inhabitants of the kingdom belonged to the ethnic group of the Fon. These were not very popular among the neighboring peoples because of the constant wars for obtaining slaves. Every few years a new war was opened to obtain new slaves, who were sometimes put to work in the kingdom itself, and sometimes sold to European slave traders. To better control the slave trade, the kingdoms of Allada and Savi were occupied in 1724 and 1727. These lay between the kingdom and the sea and hindered direct trade with the Europeans.

The Trans-Atlantic slave trade

The Atlantic slave trade did not come out of nowhere. For centuries there had been trade in slaves in Africa, Africans sold captured prisoners of war to African and Arab traders. During the fifteenth and sixteenth centuries, the need for forced labor grew in Europe, especially in the then newly occupied colonies. In the late fifteenth and into the sixteenth centuries, several thousand slaves were transported from Africa each year.

The need for labor on the sugar and tobacco plantations in the new colonies in the Americas and the shortage of free labor from Europe drove the Trans-Atlantic slave trade ever higher. Around the middle of the seventeenth century - when sugar cultivation was well developed in the Caribbean - the slave trade exploded. By 1700, fifty thousand slaves were being transported each year. The proceeds brought increased prosperity to Europe and a way to better balance the trade balance with Asia. With the development of the Atlantic system, it contributed greatly to European expansion and thus to the development of capitalism.

(a historic illustration depicting the kidnapping of slaves)

However, this was accompanied by great human tragedies. Over the centuries, slave hunters enslaved tens of millions of people, many of whom made the Trans-Atlantic journey to North and South America and the Caribbean. Many died before they could be sold for transport; it is estimated that between eleven and fourteen million slaves were shipped to the West during this diaspora. On average, about 15% of the slaves died during the journey.

On the societies of Africa, the Trans-Atlantic slave trade had a disruptive effect whereby it is known to this day which ancestors were slave hunters. Not only did the slave trade represent a significant drain on the population in Africa, it also dramatically changed the societies there by promoting the militarization of African societies and slavery in Africa itself. In addition, slavery contributed to the reinforcement of racism by seeking a justification for slavery that had previously been portrayed as immoral by Christianity.

The study of the Trans-Atlantic slave trade has had its own development. The earliest works are those of British abolitionists who emphasized the cruel nature of the trade in order to garner support for the abolition of the slave trade. In addition to this moral approach, several perspectives have since been added. For example, the Trans-Atlantic slave trade is also examined from the business side, its impact on capitalism, European imperialism, the creation of an Atlantic world, its social and cultural consequences, the part played by African slave hunters, and the source of racism in the New World.

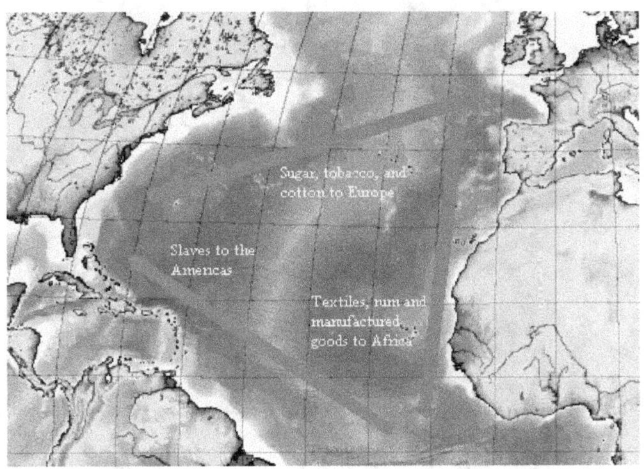

(Trans-Atlantic triangular trade)

The triangular trade or triangular navigation was the trade between Europe, America, and Africa. Ships departed from Western Europe with as their trade goods mainly firearms, gunpowder, iron, and textiles. These were exchanged for slaves, gold, and ivory in West Africa with local rulers and African and Arab slave traders.

From West Africa, ships carrying slaves then departed through the Middle Passage for North America or the Caribbean. The conditions of the slaves during the voyage were miserable and many died. The slaves were sold in America as plantation workers. Ships left North America and the Caribbean for Western Europe carrying luxury goods such as sugar, rum, coffee, cotton, silver, and tobacco.

(The Flag of the West India Company)

The trade was conducted by the Dutch West India Company, among others. Trade between the Netherlands and the Atlantic world came about through the West India Company's great offensive against the Iberian superpowers, the Portuguese power in the South Atlantic and against the Spanish Caribbean.

After obtaining the monopoly on the Atlantic trade, the West India Company became the main trader on the Gold Coast, where the Company operated from Fort Nassau in Ghana. Also, the fort was used for the trade in grain of paradise and ivory. North of the Gold Coast, the West India Company traded in Senegal, Gambia, and Sierra Leone. Elmina was still owned by the Portuguese.

In the next chapter we'll dive deeper into why the Trans-Atlantic slave trade was set up. What the conditions and motivations were behind this gruesome part of history.

(a Dutch painting of ships from that time period engaged in battle)

Chapter 3: The reasons for the Trans-Atlantic slave trade

The climate in Europe was less suitable for the cultivation of a number of crops. Tropical and subtropical Africa was more satisfactory for this reason, but the interior, with its tropical forests and parasites, was for a long time difficult to traverse, while rivers such as the Congo and the Niger were difficult or impossible for ocean-going vessels to navigate. On the edge of the desert where agriculture was possible, states were already present that were too strong to colonize. A good alternative was initially the Atlantic islands and later the New World. The Aztecs and the Incas were the most important civilizations here. The heart of the former was in Mexico, but its cultural influence reached as far as the Mississippi River. The empire of the Incas stretched from southern Colombia to northern Chile and Argentina. In these well-organized parts of the Americas, the Spanish were able to quickly assume authority. In the areas beyond, where there had been no central government, this was a much more difficult process. This was the case with the Maya in Yucatán, but also in Brazil and North America.

(Indigenous people and colonists in North America)

Before the large-scale mechanization of the Industrial Revolution, people relied primarily on human labor. However, it was not a foregone conclusion that this would be slaves and that these slaves would come from Africa. Initially, labor was drawn from the local population. In the area of the Aztecs and the Incas, they could use the existing system to recruit large numbers of workers and there was no need to switch to slavery. Nor would this have been in keeping with the desire to Christianize this population. The Portuguese did initially try to make use of the local population, but they had little experience with agriculture and with the lack of a central authority they therefore proved unable to employ sufficient labor force. Also, the population in their assigned areas was too small to support the plantation economy.

Added to this was the fact that the local population was unfamiliar with a number of diseases that had a very devastating effect. In the Old World these had mostly been transmitted through contact with domesticated herd animals. There, too, this had claimed many victims, but a certain degree of immunity had been built up over the centuries. America now had to deal with a whole range of these diseases in a short period of time, with the population also having a smaller genetic variation. At least 50% and possibly 90% of the local population lost their lives between 1492 and 1650, making this the largest population disaster in history with the fourteenth-century epidemics in Eurasia.

From Europe, it was difficult to get labor toward the New World, which had several causes. First, while economic growth was low at less than 0.25% per year by today's standards, it was considerably higher than previous periods. This meant that in Europe itself there was a great demand for labor, the supply of which was still relatively low due to the great famine and the Black Death of the fourteenth century. Certainly, Portugal, with less than a million inhabitants, could barely manage its empire, let alone provide sufficient labor. Although Spain had a population of over seven million, it had a European empire to defend, which required more and more soldiers. Therefore, despite the presence of precious metals, the opportunities in Europe and the dangers of the New World made it unattractive for the poor population to move away. When there was an insufficient supply of free labor, they turned to slavery.

As long as labor was scarcer than land, this encouraged serfdom and slavery. This was the case during the Early Middle Ages in Europe. Slaves would be the cheapest from Europe, which had previously been the case with the Slavic peoples. These were used by Venice in Crete and Cyprus, among others, to exploit sugarcane plantations using techniques adopted from Syria. However, the rise of the Ottoman Empire blocked Slavic resources.

In Western Europe, slavery largely disappeared during the Middle Ages, partly due to Christianization and economic causes. Around the Mediterranean this was not the case. In fact, with the Arab conquests, there was an increase in the slave trade here. In the rest of Africa, too, labor was scarce, and wealth was measured by the number of people under it. The slave trade in Africa therefore took place at least a thousand years before the Europeans became involved. Until then, however, it was modest in scale.

People hardly ever enslaved members of their own society and in Europe most states were too powerful to be able to obtain slaves on a large scale. This was not the case in Africa, where certain peoples could more easily dominate and enslave other societies. The Europeans therefore joined a network of Arab slave trade that had existed for at least six centuries. The slaves were supplied by African and Arab traders and brought to the Americas by the Europeans. The high costs of purchasing the slaves, the passage and the suppression of rebellions were initially financed by the first source of income from the New World, the gold and silver mines. At a later stage, the income from the plantations was also used for this purpose.

(Colonization of the Americas by Britain)

Chapter 4: The history of the Trans-Atlantic slave trade

In 1415, as an extension of the Reconquista, the Portuguese conquered the rich Ceuta. This was the terminus of trade caravans from West Africa, and after the conquest this source dried up, and they decided to take over the trade themselves. The trade in slaves began in 1444, but was initially secondary to their main commodity from Africa, gold.

Slaves were used in Portugal for domestic chores, and in Portugal's southern port cities they eventually made up to 15% of the total population. In other Portuguese and Spanish port cities, they could be as high as 10%. In addition, the Portuguese participated in trade along the African coast to finance gold. This situation changed when the Portuguese began to operate sugar cane plantations on Madeira in 1455. This changed the need for slaves who were now employed on these plantations. Initially, these slaves were obtained mainly from Senegambia and the Gold Coast.

This changed when sugar plantations were also exploited on Sao Tome and Principe and the Portuguese entered into an alliance with the Kingdom of Congo. The societies found in Africa proved too powerful to colonize, so the search for more land for sugar plantations was one of the driving forces to look for increasingly western islands.

In the New World, the plantation system was copied from the Atlantic islands, but on a much larger scale. Thus, in the New World, a plantation economy emerged with wealthy European owners from the sugar industry at the head who owned many slaves and sugar fields. Among them were the planters who could not afford a sugar mill. Poor peasants as in Europe were virtually non-existent. For this group there were only administrative positions and specific jobs in the sugar mills.

The majority of the population consisted of the slaves who did the heavy work. Initially, the acculturated and Christianized slaves (negros ladinos) from the Iberian Peninsula were used here, but soon they were brought directly from Africa (negros bocales). Ferdinand II of Aragon authorized Bartolomeo Marchionni to transport the first slaves from Africa to the Americas (Santo Domingo) in 1510. Emperor Charles V granted a license to Laurent de Gorrevod in 1518 for the tax-free transfer of 4,000 African slaves to his American possessions. The banking house Welser received the next major license in 1528. Spain could not establish settlements in Africa itself due to the 1494 Treaty of Tordesillas, so it granted Portugal an exclusive asiento in 1595.

Brazil

In 1500, Brazil was discovered by Portugal and, according to the Treaty of Tordesillas, the area came to them as well. The riches brought by trade with the Spice Islands and India meant that colonization of Brazil was not a priority for the first few decades. This changed when the French and British began to settle in the area. Portugal then set about the colonization and to finance it they used the tried-and-true method of sugar plantations. The first arrived around 1550 and soon the productivity here was higher than in the Atlantic islands. From 1560 there was a continuous slave trade on Brazil.

In exchange for support, Álvaro I of Congo gave the Portuguese the right to settle south of his kingdom. Luanda was founded there in 1576 and from then on, most slaves shipped to the Americas would come from Angola.

While the Portuguese supplied the slaves, the transport of sugar to Europe was in the hands of the Dutch. Antwerp thus became the center of the European sugar market. This changed during the Eighty Years' War, when the Dutch came up against the Spaniards. This did not directly affect relations with Portugal, but in 1580 Portugal was annexed to Spain after the Battle of Alcântara. The war with Spain and Portugal also deprived the Netherlands of the profitable spice trade. This was an incentive to expand shipping beyond Europe, and a century after the Portuguese, the Dutch found the route to Asia.

(Portuguese ships arriving in Brazil)

As a result, they soon clashed with the Portuguese. As a result, a de facto Portuguese-Dutch War was fought as a global extension of the Eighty Years' War. In the fight against the Spaniards and the Portuguese, privateering was used in the beginning. This was the main source of income of the West India Company (WIC) just after its founding in 1621. Then the WIC developed the Groot Desseyn, a large plan in which the Portuguese sugar trade from Brazil was to be undermined by taking over the slave trade.

With the capture of the Silver Fleet in 1628, sufficient funds were available. Between 1630 and 1634 Recife with a large part of the Brazilian coast was conquered, this became Dutch Brazil. In 1637 the island of Elmina near the Gold Coast was conquered, the major Portuguese slave trading stronghold. For the following centuries, this fortress would be one of the centers of the slave trade of the WIC. In 1641 Luanda was also conquered from the Portuguese. By 1700, the WIC owned about a dozen forts on the West African coast.

After this, the Dutch slave trade began to take on large proportions. To maintain sugar production, many Portuguese plantation owners were able to keep their plantations. From Dutch Brazil, however, many techniques were transferred to the rest of the Americas, ending the Brazilian sugar monopoly.

This paved the way for the establishment of French and English colonies in the Americas. Beginning in 1640, the slave trade with Brazil began to collapse and trade was shifted to the Spanish colonies in the Americas. Initially, Dutch traders transported slaves to Buenos Aires and Rio de la Plata in what is now Argentina; later, the Caribbean also became a target of the slave trade.

In 1654, Brazil was reconquered by Portugal after which sugar cane cultivation was transferred to the Caribbean, causing Brazil to lose its monopoly and start an economic decline. This had its effect on the number of slaves brought to Brazil until gold was discovered in Minas Gerais in 1695. This greatly increased the slave trade.

Caribbean

After the Portuguese reconquest of Brazil, Curaçao, captured in 1634, became the Dutch collection point for slaves. After the English conquest of Jamaica in 1655, it became an important transit market of slaves for the Spanish colonies. At first, the Caribbean was mostly home to tobacco plantations, but later sugar plantations became similar in size to those in Brazil.

From 1641, sugar was exported from here to Europe. New buyers were found in the English and French who grew tobacco on the islands they conquered in the Caribbean and in Virginia. Until about 1660, the French and English depended on the Dutch to develop and supply these colonies with slaves, but as their role in Asia grew, so did their role in the slave trade. The English wars in which the French assisted the English ended Dutch hegemony, and by the end of the seventeenth century the English and French had a significant share in the Atlantic slave trade.

The English had been involved in the slave trade since 1562 with John Hawkins playing a pioneering role. From 1672 the Royal African Company had a monopoly on the slave trade but lost it in 1698. Then in the eighteenth century the slave trade increased enormously. There were years when more than one hundred thousand slaves were transported. However, France and England took over the position of the Republic, as they did with the other trade. The French used Saint-Domingue in particular for this purpose, which they obtained in 1697 with the Treaty of Rijswijk.

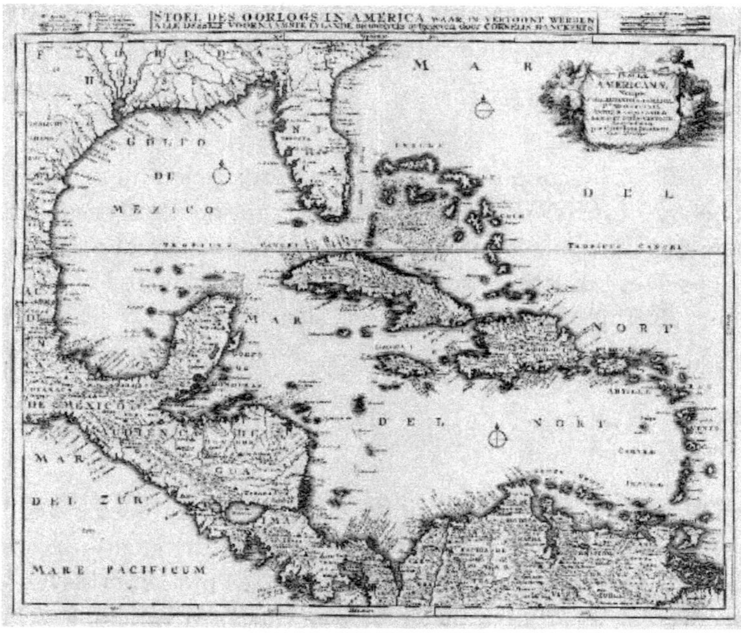

(a map of the Caribbean during that time period)

North America

The English colonies in North America were from shortly after their inception a destination for African slaves, in addition to the Indians whom the colonists themselves enslaved.

The colony of Jamestown in Virginia, founded in 1607, purchased the first shipment of black slaves in 1619. This was about twenty people brought by the White Lion, a privateer from Flushing that had intercepted the Portuguese slave ship São João Bautista, but now desperately needed food. The resulting exchange is considered the beginning of black slavery in the United States, which would last until 1865. Beginning in the 1680s, the slave trade from Africa really began to take off and the plantation economy took off.

(the establishment of new Amsterdam in North America)

Chapter 5: Slavery during the Trans-Atlantic slave trade

Slavery existed in various forms and degrees, in which self-determination was limited to a greater or lesser degree. Initially, a large part of the population in the American colonies consisted of contract workers, mostly European, but also African. In this, they retained a right of self-determination to some degree and normally regained freedom after some time. For Africans, debt bondage could be one of the reasons for having to make the Atlantic crossing. However, whereas even with debt bondage some degree of self-determination is still possible, and one could buy oneself free again, with Trans-Atlantic slavery the dehumanization was further implemented. This was a case of chattel slavery, where the owner had almost unlimited power.

(the drowning of slaves during this period)

Slave rebellions

Slave rebellions occurred both in Africa, during the journey, and in the Americas. Probably about 10% of the voyages involved rebellions. Rebellions were especially high on voyages from Upper Guinea (Senegambia, Sierra Leone, and the Ivory Coast), so residents of this coast made up a relatively small portion of the total number of slaves.

In the New World there were many rebellions, such as the Berbice slave rebellions in 1763 and the Curaçao slave rebellion of 1795 led by Tula. Generally, however, these were put down. Only the Haitian Revolution of 1791 to 1804 was successful in driving out the slave owners. In addition, many slaves ran away and then organized themselves into Maroon communities.

(Illustrated slave rebellions)

The effects of slavery

Although slave trading in Africa existed before the Europeans intervened in it, the scale on which it took place thereafter was considerably larger.

While the earlier numbers were not inconsiderable, the demographic impact was limited, and societies did not change significantly. This changed with the Atlantic slave trade. Politically, the influence was also great. It triggered a militarization of African societies that led to state formation in which aggressive states such as Ashanti and Dahomey were at an advantage, while peoples such as the Yoruba, Benin, and the Mossi eventually went into decline. Economically it encouraged short-term solutions, while socially it led to division, where to this day one knows which ancestors were slave hunters.

The Atlantic slave trade also had the effect of increasing the internal slave trade in Africa to the point that there are estimates that at the height of the slave trade there may have been as many slaves in Africa as in the Americas. As the Trans-Atlantic slave trade waned, slaves in Africa became cheaper and the number actually increased until there were more slaves in Africa than in the Americas.

In the Americas, slaves replaced locals who succumbed to diseases unknown to them. Until the nineteenth century, Brazil had the largest slave population, after which this position was taken over by the United States.

First, historian Williams brought up how the slave trade and slavery had contributed to European prosperity and expansion. In Capitalism and Slavery from 1944, he argued that slavery had made a significant contribution to early capitalism and financed the Industrial Revolution. Subsequently, that same revolution and the resulting industrial capitalism made slavery obsolete.

Williams also countered the then prevailing notion that abolitionism stemmed primarily from humanitarian concerns. For example, he argued that if Pitt had been successful in conquering Saint-Domingue, it would have abandoned abolitionism, since Saint-Domingue - where 40,000 slaves had to be brought in each year to keep the sugarcane plantations running - would have no value without slaves. Here he formulated what would become known as the Williams thesis, the economic necessity of slavery to make the industrial revolution possible, which would then make slavery unprofitable:

The commercial capitalism of the eighteenth century developed the wealth of Europe by means of slavery and monopoly. But in so doing it helped to create the industrial capitalism of the nineteenth century, which turned round and destroyed the power of commercial capitalism, slavery, and all its works. Without a grasp of these economic changes the history of the period is meaningless.

This Williams thesis has since become the subject of much debate, but there seem to be strong indications that the thesis may not hold up in its entirety, but at least in important respects. It has been argued against the thesis that the economic importance and profitability of the slave trade was minimal for Europe.

However, this leaves aside the fact that slavery was very important in making the colonization of the Americas possible and thus set in motion a development of European expansion coupled with the development of new financial instruments.

It was also Williams who argued that racism stemmed primarily from slavery through the need for justification and the dehumanization that preceded it.

The morality of slavery in that time period

The above cases make it seem as if only business considerations were at play here. However, there was a realization that one was going against human values and norms here.

Motives such as the pursuit of profit and the weakening of the enemy, however, pushed this awareness into the background. For example, the Roman Catholic Church initially discouraged enslavement, but with the Romanus Pontifex of 1455, authorized the enslavement of non-Christians as a missionary activity.

The treatment of the Indians in the New World created critical voices in Spain, especially through the work of priest Las Casas who was supported by the influential Cisneros.

Las Casas particularly opposed the system of encomienda and played an important role in the creation of the New Laws, Las Nuevas Leyes de las Indias. In 1542, this curbed the exploitation of Indians, although it could not completely eliminate custom. Nor could it prevent the large-scale extraction of slaves from Africa.

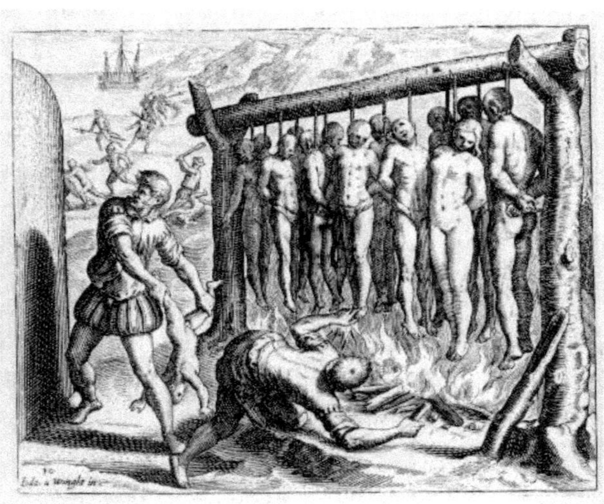

(The drawing of "The Brevísima relación of 1552" by priest Las Casas)

Chapter 6: The abolition of the Trans-Atlantic slave trade

Opposition to slavery grew over the centuries and abolitionism became a major movement, especially in England. The Quakers were the first to oppose slavery because it was said to be unchristian. Under the influence of the Enlightenment and the idea of human rights, the movement expanded.

Alexander Falconbridge sailed as a physician on several voyages and became an abolitionist there.

His An Account of the Slave Trade on the Coast of Africa from 1788 would become an important influence in abolitionism:

During the voyages I made, I was frequently a witness to the fatal effects of this exclusion of the fresh air. I will give one instance, as it serves to convey some idea, though a very faint one, of the sufferings of those unhappy beings whom we wantonly drag from their native country, and doom to perpetual labor and captivity. Some wet and blowing weather having occasioned the portholes to be shut, and the grating to be covered, fluxes and fevers among the negroes ensued. While they were in this situation, I frequently went down among them, until at length their apartments became so extremely hot, as to be only sufferable for a very short time.

But the excessive heat was not the only thing that rendered their situation intolerable. The deck, that is, the floor of their rooms, was so covered with the blood and mucus which had proceeded from them in consequence of the flux, that it resembled a slaughterhouse. It is not in the power of the human imagination, to picture to itself a situation more dreadful or disgusting.

Numbers of the slaves having fainted, they were carried upon deck, where several of them died, and the rest were, with great difficulty, restored. It had nearly proved fatal to me also.

The climate was too warm to admit the wearing of any clothing but a shirt, and that I had pulled off before I went down; notwithstanding which, by only continuing among them for about a quarter of an hour, I was so overcome with the heat, stench, and foul air, that I had nearly fainted; and it was not without assistance, that I could get upon deck. The consequence was, that I soon after fell sick of the same disorder, from which I did not recover for several months.

The Danes banned the slave trade in 1803, followed by the British with the Slave Trade Act of March 25, 1807. However, according to Thomas Clarkson, an important British abolitionist, the British would never have made it this far without the American Revolution:

As long as America was our own, there was no chance that a minister would have attended to the groans of the sons and daughters of Africa, however he might feel for their distress.

Clarkson (1788): ***An Essay on the Impolicy of the African Slave Trade***

In 1808, the United States introduced a ban on the importation of new slaves from Africa (Act Prohibiting Importation of Slaves). Sales of slaves born within the U.S. would remain possible for another half century.

After the British ban on the slave trade, the Trans-Atlantic slave trade nevertheless continued for several decades, as a kind of stealth trade, with Brazil being the main destination. It was only when the British navy began to combat this clandestine trade with sharper patrols in the mid-nineteenth century that this gradually came to an end.

British Foreign Secretary Lord Castlereagh negotiated the issue with plenipotentiaries from Portugal and Spain on the margins of the Congress of Vienna in 1815. This led to a treaty with Portugal in which it was agreed that no more Portuguese nationals would buy slaves along the West African coast north of the equator. In return, Britain repaid Portugal a debt of £600,000, the remainder of a loan taken out by the Portuguese government in 1809. In 1833, Britain officially abolished slavery with a Slavery Abolition Act.

A number of countries followed, often under British pressure, but where the economic importance of slavery was still great, there was great resistance. In the United States, so much so that it led to the American Civil War (1861-65). However, mechanization reduced the scarcity of labor, while slave rebellions could be such a cost that slavery became more expensive than paid labor. In Africa, slavery had actually grown after the Trans-Atlantic slave trade came to an end. Ironically, the subsequent drop in prices made slavery affordable in Africa.

Williams brought an alternative explanation. It was not a growing morality, but economic drivers that underpinned abolition, just as they had contributed to its emergence. After capitalism had been able to develop in part because of slavery to the point that the industrial revolution became possible, that same revolution made slavery uneconomic. Just as racism intensified with growing slavery, morality increased as slavery became less economically beneficial. About the then prevailing colonial historiography, he later stated:

The British historians wrote almost as if Britain had introduced slavery solely for the satisfaction of abolishing it. They have made such play of the compensation provided by Britain to the planters as wiping off the debt to the West Indians in respect of slavery that it is difficult not to see in this attitude, developed and propagated over a century and a quarter, the explanation of the British Government's attitude on economic aid to the West Indies and on preferential treatment of the West Indies sugar industry.

These are political conclusions. As such they are a legitimate reply to the political conclusions drawn by the British historians themselves.

The desirability of abolishing slavery emerged strongly during the Enlightenment period, when notions of liberty, equality, and civil and human rights were gaining ground. Important thinkers on this subject were Jean-Jacques Rousseau in France and Thomas Jefferson in the United States.

Williams brought an alternative explanation. It was not a growing morality, but economic drivers that underpinned abolition, just as they had contributed to its emergence. After capitalism had been able to develop in part because of slavery to the point that the Industrial Revolution became possible, that same revolution made slavery uneconomic. Just as racism intensified with growing slavery, morality increased as slavery became less economically beneficial. About the then prevailing colonial historiography, he later stated:

The British historians wrote almost as if Britain had introduced slavery solely for the satisfaction of abolishing it. They have made such play of the compensation provided by Britain to the planters as wiping off the debt to the West Indians in respect of slavery that it is difficult not to see in this attitude, developed and propagated over a century and a quarter, the explanation of the British Government's attitude on economic aid to the West Indies and on preferential treatment of the West Indies sugar industry.

These are political conclusions. As such they are a legitimate reply to the political conclusions drawn by the British historians themselves.

The economic transformation of capitalism toward wage labor and away from mercantilism was thus a factor in the abandonment of slavery. However, the plantation economy remained profitable for longer than many historians assumed, leading to a renewed emphasis on moral and ideological motives in the early 21st century. In the process, much attention was focused on slave revolts as the driving force behind abolition, with the most imaginative example being that of the French colony of Saint Domingue in 1793. This Haitian Revolution, which could not be contained by military force, led to the outlawing of slavery on the island.

The development overseas was the signal for the French revolutionaries to give effect to their ideals of liberty, equality, and fraternity in 1794, and to the first article of the Declaration of the Rights of Man and the Citizen, by putting an end to slavery in all territories under French rule. Napoleon Bonaparte reversed the achievement in 1802 in an attempt to get the colonies to contribute to the Napoleonic Wars. Mee to thwart this plan, the United Kingdom banned the slave trade in 1807, as Denmark had done in 1803. The United States also banned the import and export of slaves in 1808. The Netherlands, France, and partially Portugal followed suit in 1814-1815. In all these powers, the keeping of slaves remained legitimate.

The issue of abolishing the slave trade also came up indirectly at the Congress of Vienna. British Foreign Secretary Lord Castlereagh (who had moral objections) and Tsar Alexander I favored it. The plenipotentiaries of Spain (Labrador) and Portugal (Palmella) opposed it, arguing that the prohibition of the slave trade had profound effects on their economies, respectively in Cuba and Brazil, which could not spare the slaves as cheap labor. Palmella also cited the issue that it was not covered by international law and was an internal matter of each country. He reminded Congress that the abolition of the slave trade was not the issue here. Castlereagh then raised the idea of trade sanctions on goods produced by slave labor. This led to some spiteful reactions. The matter was finally shelved with solemn declarations branding slave trade as repugnant and immoral. They expressed their desire to eradicate the slave trade and promised to pursue that goal with zeal and perseverance. The Spanish Empire banned slave trade starting in 1820.

A new phase began in which the institution of slavery itself came under pressure. The end of slavery was included in the new constitution that Mexico adopted in 1824. The British Empire took the step in 1833, after major uprisings in Jamaica and elsewhere. The controversial transitional measure of "apprenticeship" was lifted in 1838, removing the last formal barrier to freedom. However, slaves who did not find free land often remained employed by their former owners. In 1848, reintroduced slavery in French colonies was banned and the Code Noir abolished.

In 1859, the Netherlands abolished slavery in the directly administered parts of the East Indies. A strategic moment by Minister of Colonies Jan Jacob Rochussen. One year later, Max Havelaar, Multatuli's (Eduard Douwes Dekker) indictment of Dutch policy in the Dutch East Indies, was published.

Another four years later, in 1863, the Netherlands abolished lucrative slavery in the West Indian colonies (Suriname and the Dutch Antilles). In Europe, the Netherlands was among the mid-range of countries that abolished slavery. Denmark, the United Kingdom and France had preceded the Netherlands, but countries like Portugal, Spain, Italy, Iceland, Bulgaria, and present-day Turkey followed suit (much) later. Globally, the Netherlands was among the leading countries in abolishing slavery.

(The official plaque of the British Anti-Slavery Society)

The United States came out with President Lincoln's Emancipation Proclamation in September 1862, when abolition of slavery had become inevitable as one of the war's aims during the American Civil War. On January 1, 1863, abolition took effect in the northern states. General slave strikes contributed to the southern defeat. In the end, Matilda McCrear was the last survivor when she died in 1940,[82] and the United States was the last to do so.

Portugal and Spain did so even later, arguing that their economies depended on slavery. In the Portuguese colonies the official end came in 1869 and in the Spanish in 1886.

In Brazil in 1888, during the absence of Emperor Pedro, Princess Isabella signed the Lei de Aurea abolishing slavery. It would cost Pedro his throne.

The Brussels Convention in 1890 criminalized the trade in African slaves. This put the Arab slave trade in particular in the spotlight. The Ottoman Empire abolished slavery in 1890, the last partly European country, but in some places the phenomenon continued into the early 20th century.

In some parts of Africa and Asia, including Liberia, Ethiopia, Arabia, and the indirectly administered parts of the Dutch East Indies, slavery remained legitimate into the 20th century; on the island of Sumbawa (now Sumbawa, Indonesia), slaves were freed on March 31, 1910, and on the island of Samosir not until 1914. 83][84] In Ethiopia, slavery was abolished in 1931, in Bahrain in 1937, in Kuwait in 1949, in Qatar in 1952, and in Yemen in 1962.

In the latter year, Crown Prince Faisal of Saudi Arabia released some 100,000 to 200,000 East African slaves. The 1970 coup by Qaboes also abolished slavery in Oman. In 1981, slavery was officially abolished in Mauritania, making Mauritania the last slave state in the world. Slavery did not become punishable in Mauritania until 2007.

International Treaties

One of the first international treaties to abolish slavery in Africa was the Brussels Convention of 1890. After World War I, the Brussels General Act was adapted by the Convention of Saint-Germain-en-Laye (1919) and later replaced by the International Slavery Convention (1926) within the framework of the League of Nations. That convention was supplemented in 1956 by the Supplementary Convention on the Abolition of Slavery, under the United Nations.

In addition, a variety of human rights treaties exist that directly or indirectly counteract forms of slavery or extreme exploitation. In labor law, a Convention Concerning Forced or Compulsory Labor, 1930 (No.29) on forced labor (1930), supplemented in 2014 by an amended protocol, applies within the International Labor Organization.

Article 4 of the 1948 Universal Declaration of Human Rights states that no one shall be held in slavery or serfdom and that slavery, and the slave trade are prohibited in all forms.

The emergence of generally applicable legislation, including on slavery, together with the idea of freedom, would lead over the centuries to the development of the principle of equality and thus to calls for the abolition of slavery. An important statement already formed the preambles of the American Declaration of Independence and the U.S. Constitution.

Chapter 7: The statistics of the Trans-Atlantic slave trade

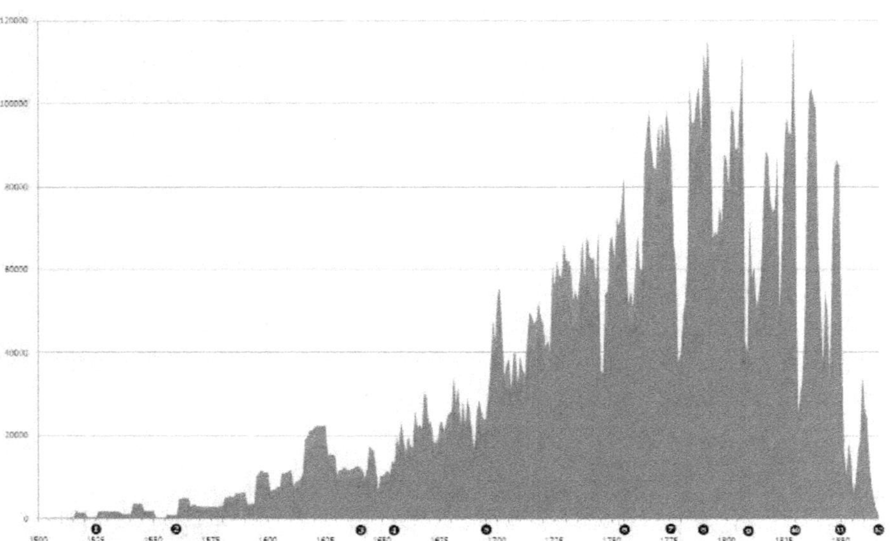

(The estimated number of shipped slaves during the period of 1525 – 1867)

Thus, mostly African slave hunters managed to enslave millions of people over the centuries. Many died before they could be sold for transport, but between eleven and fourteen million were shipped to the Americas. The largest numbers went to Brazil and the Caribbean, about 40% each, while about 5% ended up in the United States.

Until 1600, about a quarter of the slaves left Africa via the Atlantic slave trade, while the rest left the continent via the Sahara and Red Sea ports. After that, the route via the Atlantic Ocean became larger than that of North and East Africa. By 1700, slaves were even Africa's main export product.

The Portuguese learned early on to use the winds and sea currents, called volta do mar. In both the northern and southern hemispheres there is a gyre, a main circulation or circuit of sea currents.

Near Brazil lies the South Atlantic gyre which made the route to Angola a favorable one. The vast majority of slaves for Brazil therefore came from there with Luanda as the main port, but also from the Bay of Benin with Ouidah as the main port and Southeast Africa and slaves were taken. Slaves destined for the Caribbean and North America were mainly taken from West Africa via the North Atlantic gyre, especially from the bays of Benin and Biafra and the Gold Coast.

Estimates of the slave-trade statistics

Where archives on ship voyages are lacking, estimates are usually no more than that, estimates of an often-speculative nature, just as, incidentally, estimates of the development of the world's population are speculative in the absence of censuses. The most accurate estimates of the Trans-Atlantic slave trade are those of the Voyages database of Emory University, which combines data from several national archives. However, even this approach has its problems in those different countries each used a separate system, so that a ship arriving in a different jurisdiction than the one from which it left sometimes had more people on board than it left with.

Estimates of trade through the Sahara, Red Sea and Indian Ocean are many times more inaccurate. These estimates are mostly based on Austen's work. In his latest work, he assumes about ten million people for the period 800-1900. Estimates from before 1600 are particularly imprecise and can vary from two-thirds to double that number. Only the numbers from the nineteenth century are somewhat reliable, but not yet of the level of data on the Trans-Atlantic slave trade. The number of slaves in Africa itself is highly speculative, with Manning arriving at a figure of about eight million.

An early estimate of the number of people who made the forced crossing from Africa was that of a total of just under fourteen million by Dunbar in his 1863 History of the Rise and Decline of Commercial Slavery in America. An influential work was that by Kuczynski, who in 1936 arrived at almost fifteen million people.

However, he based himself on Du Bois, who in turn based himself on the unknown Dunbar in his work The Negro from 1915, but had rounded up. Du Bois himself set the lower limit at ten million. Although these were very rough unsubstantiated estimates, despite the criticism this range proved to be in line with later work. The same is not true for the number of people who would have died during the journey, where Du Bois assumed five out of six and thus arrived at sixty million people who had been carried out of Africa.

Curtin was highly critical of the facile way in which the figure of fifteen million had taken on a life of its own, with historians quoting each other so that Dunbar's origins had become completely unclear. Curtin's 1969 work was an important impetus in arriving at a good estimate of the number of slaves who made the crossing. His estimate of 9.566 million slaves was considered too low by Inikori, who himself arrived at about 15.4 million people. Many scientists, including Lovejoy in 1982, refined this over the years.

Over the years, different types of datasets of slave travel emerged, mostly based on a single country or port. By chance, David Eltis and Stephen Behrendt met in 1990 at the Public Record Office while independently researching the British slave trade. It was there that the idea of combining the databases arose. In the years that followed, the data was standardized and reconciled, and in 1999 a CD-ROM was issued containing 27,233 voyages. In the years that followed, the database was further expanded, especially with trips from Latin America that were still missing. In 2006 this became available online via Voyages: The Trans-Atlantic Slave Trade Database at Emory University. This database now contains nearly 36,000 slave voyages. Estimates on the numbers of people who were captured and died before crossing are much less accurate.

Mortality rates of the slave-trade

On average, about 15% of slaves died during the voyage, but this varied greatly by region of Africa, season, and the number of slaves on board. Gastroenterological diseases such as dysentery were the main cause, followed by fever. Although slaves were not cheap and it was therefore rewarding for slave traders to get them across alive, more died than crew members during the middle passage. After 1790, the mortality rate on British ships declined sharply, possibly due to the Dolben's Act of 1788 which placed limits on the number of slaves that could be taken.

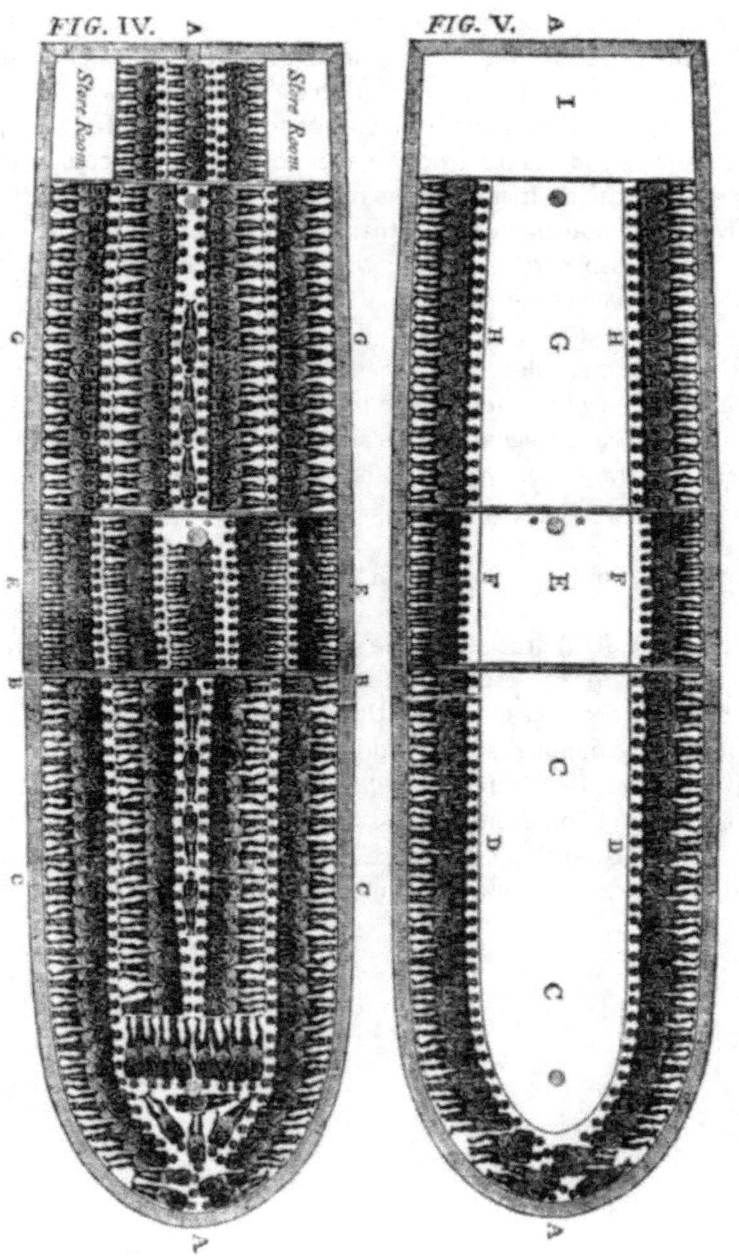

(Schematic drawing of a slave ship used during this period)

While the average death rate for the crew on middle passage was lower than that for the slaves, for the entire triangle the rate was higher for the mostly ill-treated and not always voluntary crew as well. This was a result of the longer voyage with the trip from Europe to Africa, the stay there, the middle passage and the trip from America to Europe. This could vary greatly by destination in Africa, with the mortality rate of voyages to the Gambia River being noticeably higher than those to the Gold Coast, while the mortality rate also increased during the rainy season. Yellow fever and malaria were the main causes of death.

The majority of the crew died on the coastal voyage and on the crossing to America, but even when they arrived there a considerable number died. The surgeon was at higher risk because of his direct contact with both slaves and crew. According to Thomas Clarkson, a ship lost about 20-25% of its crew during the entire voyage.

International Year for People of African Descent

The United Nations (UN) proclaimed the year 2011 as the "International Year for People of African Descent. In doing so, the UN wanted to focus attention on the African Diaspora. The UN also wants to use the Declaration to force member states to do some self-examination regarding the Durban Declaration and Plan of Action (DDPA). This was decided at the World Conference Against Racism (WCAR) in Durban, South Africa, in 2001. At that conference it was recognized that slavery and the slave trade are and always should have been crimes against humanity.

Chapter 8: The tragedy of Belgian Congo

Beginning in the 1870s, the Congo interior was first explored by Europeans, such as David Livingstone. The Welsh American explorer Henry Morton Stanley went in search of him and mapped the area for the first time. King Leopold II of Belgium employed him to realize his colonial ambitions. From the west coast, Stanley occupied the territory by establishing posts for the Comité d'études du Haut-Congo and the Association internationale du Congo. In 1885, the land was granted to Leopold II at the Berlin Conference. He ruled as king-sovereign over this Congo Free State, where he installed a reign of terror. The Swahilo-Arab caravan trade in slaves and ivory was taken over by force of arms, with slavery largely replaced by forced labor. Financially, the loss-making colony kept its head above water thanks to loans from the Belgian state. From 1895, the Congo state brought in a fortune for the monarch thanks to the export of rubber for the new bicycles and cars. Much of the money Leopold used for prestigious buildings in Brussels, Ostend, Tervuren and Antwerp. Meanwhile, the Congolese were exploited. Between 1885 and 1908, millions died of hunger, disease, and violence.

Crimes in Belgian Congo

Rubber became the main export product. To increase productivity, a rubber tax was introduced. Tapped rubber (latex) had to be turned in at trading posts to meet the taxes. This created a form of forced labor as companies became increasingly dependent on Congolese labor for their extraction of rubber.

The state recruited a number of black officials, known as capitas, to organize local labor. The desire to maximize rubber extraction, and thus state profits, meant that centrally enforced requirements were often arbitrary without regard to numbers or people's welfare. In the concession areas, concessionaires could use almost any measures they wanted to increase production and profits without state interference. The lack of a government to oversee commercial methods led to an atmosphere of "informality" throughout the Free State, which provoked exploitation and mistreatment. Treatment of workers (particularly the length of employment) was not regulated by law and was instead left to the discretion of officials on the ground. ABIR and the Anversoise were particularly noted for the harshness with which officials treated Congolese workers.

People who refused to tap rubber (latex) were forced out. Insurgents were beaten or whipped with the chicotte. People were taken hostage to encourage people to accelerate rubber extraction and punitive expeditions were made to destroy villages that did not cooperate. The policy led to the demise of Congolese economic and cultural life, and local agriculture came under pressure in certain areas.

Enforcement was mostly in the hands of the Force Publique, the colonial army. The Force had been established in 1885, with white officers and non-commissioned officers and black soldiers, and recruited from Zanzibar, Nigeria, and Liberia, among others. In Congo, the army recruited from specific ethnic groups and strata of the population including the Bangala. The so-called Zappo-Zaps (from the Songye ethnic group) were the most feared. The Zappo-Zaps abused their position by raiding the countryside and enslaving people. By 1900, the Force Publique numbered 19,000 men.

The rubber tax and the violent exploitation of the population that accompanied it originated with the establishment of the concession regime in 1891 and lasted until 1906 when the concession system was curtailed. At its peak, it took place mainly in the Équateur, Bandundu and Kasai regions.

(Congolese latex production slaves)

Failure to meet rubber quotas was harshly punished. In addition to imprisonment and hostage-taking, punishment could also take the form of physical violence, for example whipping with the chicotte, burning with gum, or death.

Meanwhile, the Force Publique had to provide their victims' hands as proof when they had shot and killed someone, as it was believed that otherwise they would use the ammunition (imported from Europe at considerable cost) for hunting. As a result, rubber quotas were partially repaid in severed hands. Sometimes the hands were collected by the soldiers of the Force Publique, sometimes by the villages themselves. There were even small wars where villages attacked neighboring villages to collect hands because their rubber quotas were too unrealistic to meet.

In theory, every right hand proved to be a kill. In practice, soldiers sometimes cheated by simply cutting off the hand and leaving the victim for dead. Several survivors later said they had survived a massacre by acting dead, not moving even when their hands were cut off, and waiting for the soldiers to leave before seeking help. In some cases, a soldier could shorten his tour of duty by taking more hands than the other soldiers, leading to widespread mutilations of people.

This abuse was denounced in what has been called the first international humanitarian campaign. It was driven by Protestant missionaries and by the Congo Reform Association of British journalist Edmund Dene Morel.

The writer Mark Twain and other prominent figures also spoke out. Meanwhile, pressure on the king grew within the Belgian parliament and in academic circles. The report by British diplomat Roger Casement led to the creation of the Janssens Commission, which largely confirmed the charges.

Shortly thereafter, Leopold succumbed to the pressure. After long debates, Belgium annexed the territory and took over the colony from the king as of 1908. The Colonial Charter vested legislative power in the king subject to countersignature by the Minister of Colonies. On the ground, power was exercised by the governor general.

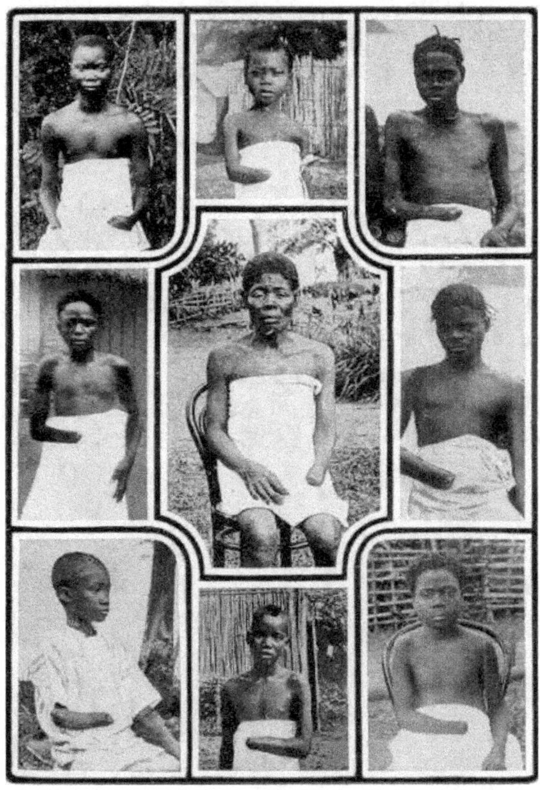

(victims of the Belgian Congo regime)

The country was now called Belgian Congo. Forced labor decreased (but did not stop), governance improved, and progress was realized in certain areas.

Congolese could receive education and medical care, but within a system of racial segregation. Moreover, a policy was pursued that excluded blacks from higher education for fear of its emancipating effect. The white colonial rulers generally exhibited a condescending, paternalistic attitude toward the indigenous population, which gave rise to resentments. On December 9, 1941, miners working at the Union Minière went on strike for better working conditions. Many strikers were slaughtered with salvos of machine guns and thrown into a mass grave. This repression, which took place during World War II, was always kept quiet in Belgium. During World War II, the Congolese army won victories against the Italians in Ethiopia.

In the 1950s, a group of évolués made some headway. Their number was estimated by the administration in 1958 at 175,000. They were Congolese who, after checks, were found to have sufficiently assimilated the Belgian culture. They enjoyed a better status than other Congolese. In 1954, the university of Lovanium opened. In a context of international decolonization, more and more Congolese began to question the Belgian regime. An economic crisis in 1959 contributed to the outbreak of riots.

Part 2: Slavery in the Americas

Chapter 1: Colonial and post-colonial slavery

So, to make a quick summary of what the events were, leading up to slavery in America.

In the previous part, we examined the events of the history of the Trans-Atlantic slave trade. During the Trans-Atlantic slave trade, predominantly black Africans were transported to North and South America. Local black chiefs in Africa offered the slaves, who enslaved them in numerous conflicts among other things. Instead of forcing these slaves to sweat themselves to death, killing them ceremonially, or selling them to Arab traders, it was more profitable to sell them to Europeans. 2,000 slaves were carried to the Americas each year from Elmina, Ghana.

They worked on the plantations there. Slavery existed in Africa prior to the arrival of the Europeans, but it was carried out on a much bigger scale afterwards as explained in the previous part of this book about the Trans-Atlantic slave trade.

The slave trade between Africa and Brazil began around 1550. It is estimated that 3 million persons, or 37 percent of all slaves in the world, ended up in this country. The Portuguese, and later the Brazilians, exploited black slaves in the (gold) mining sector, particularly on sugar cane farms, after their independence in 1822. Slavery was gradually abolished between 1850 and 1888 as a result of protests by Brazilian intellectuals and diplomatic pressure from the United Kingdom (which saw strong economic competition in cheap slave labor but also condemned slavery on humanitarian grounds).

In the process, black people were dehumanized, ridiculed, and considered as inferior and animalistic. In the transatlantic slave trade, dehumanization was a crucial component. Initially, justification for this was sought in the Bible, where, among other places, the descendants of Cham are cursed into slavery in Genesis 9 (Martin Luther thought that Cham was the origin of all brown people). Later, however, justification was mostly found by portraying the victims as inferior and savage, considerably contributing to the rise of racism.

Certain Protestant Christian groups, particularly the Quakers and Mennonites, were among the first in Europe to oppose slavery, particularly the slave trade, in the 17th century. Pietism and the Enlightenment fueled the anti-slavery movement in the 18th century. Slavery was retained in several European colonies in North and South America that obtained independence from their European home countries between 1770 and 1900, headed by European colonists. This was not the case in colonies that gained independence under non-colonial leadership, like as Haiti, where a successful black slave rebellion (1791-1804) resulted in simultaneous decolonization and abolition of slavery.

From the end of the eighteenth century, abolitionism, or anti-slavery sentiment, grew in European countries and their American ex-colonies: first, the retaining of (non-European) slaves was outlawed in Europe, though this prohibition was rarely enforced. Slavery was abolished by the French revolutionaries in 1794, but it was reinstated eight years later. After the Napoleonic Wars, the British Kingdom outlawed the slave trade, and other European governments and (former) colonies followed suit. Slavery was perpetuated in the British Empire until 1833, in the Netherlands until 1863, and in the United States until 1865, even without the slave trade.

Due of racism and the vast sums of money involved in both, opposition to the abolition of the slave trade and slavery was strong. Almost all governments compensated former slave owners when the slaves were freed. In this way, the United States is an outlier. Slaves received no compensation and were frequently forced to work after slavery was abolished.

The slave trade and slavery, according to historian Williams, contributed to European prosperity and growth. He contended in his 1944 book Capitalism and Slavery that slavery contributed significantly to early capitalism and financed the Industrial Revolution. Williams also refuted the popular belief at the time that abolitionism was largely motivated by humanitarian reasons.

For example, he claimed that if Pitt had conquered Saint-Domingue, he would have avoided abolition since Saint-Domingue, where 40,000 slaves were needed each year to keep the sugarcane fields afloat, would be worthless without them. Here he formulated the Williams thesis, or the economic necessity of slavery in order to enable the industrial revolution, which would then make slavery unprofitable.

The commercial capitalism of the eighteenth century developed the wealth of Europe by means of slavery and monopoly. But in so doing it helped to create the industrial capitalism of the nineteenth century, which turned round and destroyed the power of commercial capitalism, slavery, and all its works. Without a grasp of these economic changes the history of the period is meaningless.

Subsequently, that same revolution and the resulting industrial capitalism thus rendered slavery obsolete. This Williams thesis has subsequently become the subject of much debate, but there seem to be strong indications that the thesis may not hold up in its entirety, but at least in important respects. It has been argued against the thesis that the economic importance and profitability of the slave trade was minimal for Europe.

However, this leaves aside the fact that slavery was very important in making the colonization of the Americas possible and thus set in motion a development of European expansion coupled with the development of new financial instruments. It was also Williams who argued that racism stemmed primarily from slavery through the need for justification and the dehumanization that preceded it.

Chapter 2: Slaves in a new world

What many people might not know is that slaves in the Americas, came from many different cultures and races. To give a good perspective at the pre-face of Afro-American history, we have to take a short look at what happened during that period in time.

White slaves

Between 1512 and 1693, white slaves and enslaved women were often brought to the Caribbean, first by the Spanish, and later by others. Between 1654 and 1685, about 10,000 indentured servants, contractually obligated workers, left Bristol for the West Indies and Virginia. Some came voluntarily; others had been kidnapped on the streets of London and Bristol. Later, criminals were brought from England to the West Indies as forced laborers. French colonies had engagés. The States of Holland decided in 1684 to send criminals from the province of Holland to De West (Suriname) instead of locking them up in disciplinary houses.

Native Americans

During the colonization of the Americas, the Spanish became at war with a number of powerful civilizations, and one of the means of subduing them was to force the conquered into slave labor. The reports of Bartolomé de las Casas, a Dominican monk and historian, about the inhuman condition of the slaves found some resonance with the Spanish royal house. But above all, the alarming decimation of the native population led to the enactment of royal laws to protect the indigenous population. Plantation owners increasingly turned to Africa for slaves.

In the Spanish colony of Santo Domingo (later the capital of the Dominican Republic) the governor Ovando (from 1502) forced the Indians to work on the sugar cane plantations and in gold washing. That thousands of Indians died in the process left him cold. Each planter received the number of Indians necessary for his agriculture and gold washing.

This division of labor, called repartimiento, turned out badly for the Indians. They were forced by their masters to do very hard work, during which they were denied the necessary food. If they tried to escape their fate by fleeing into the mountains, they were pursued by bloodhounds. If they were captured, a terrible punishment awaited them. They had to work chained up as slaves. For this they had to endure the necessary flogging. Here and there the oppressed dared to resist. They were punished extremely severely for this. The heads of the rebellion(s) died under the most horrible tortures and their subordinates were forced to do the hardest labor. Many Indians died of hunger and misery. But a considerable number also took their own lives.

Asians

There were also slaves in Batavia, in the 18th century even more than 60% of the population. These had been brought in by the thousands from India and Arakan (Burma), and later also from Bali and Celebes. However, to prevent rebellions, no Javanese were allowed to be enslaved.

Africans

Around 1660, a shortage of laborers emerged in the U.S. Farmers from New Carolina and Virginia were the first to start using African slaves for the tobacco harvest. Virginia was also the first state to change its own laws: blacks who were not Christians in their homeland were considered slaves. People started importing slaves from Africa on a large scale. Black tribal leaders had discovered that it was lucrative not to kill the prisoners captured in a tribal war, as was customary at the time, but to offer them for sale at a good price.

The slaves were mainly used in the cultivation and processing of sugar cane. The life of these slaves was very hard. They were kept under their thumb with a regime of terror. The death rate on the plantations generally significantly exceeded the birth rate.

When the English, Dutch and French took possession of a large part of the Caribbean islands and the Guianas in the 17th century, they also began to establish sugarcane plantations there, using black slaves. Living conditions on the plantations were generally no better than in the United States.

Between about 1500 and 1850, about 11 million Africans were transported across the Atlantic as slaves. On average, around 15% of the slaves died in transit, similar to crew deaths. With around 550,000 slaves, the Netherlands accounted for 5% of the total transatlantic slave trade.

In the 18th century, slavery also began to develop in the English colonies along the coast of North America, the east coast of the later United States. Here the death rate among slaves was generally lower than the birth rate, perhaps due to slightly better treatment, or to the less tropical climate, which made it easier to control disease. Truly good living conditions for the black slaves here were not either.

Escaped slaves founded communities in inaccessible places. Such Maroon communities sprang up in many places, from the Amazon to the U.S. states of Florida and North Carolina. Many times, the Maroons waged a guerrilla war against the plantation owners.

Chapter 3: The United States

After the thirteen colonies on the North American east coast freed themselves from British rule during the American War of Independence (1775-1783), slavery was maintained in the United States. Several presidents such as Washington, Jefferson, Madison, Monroe, Jackson, Tyler, Polk, and Taylor kept slaves themselves on their sometimes-extensive estates during their presidencies. However, the discrepancy between this freedom of the white ex-colonists and the denial of the same right to their colored fellow men was increasingly felt, and the American abolitionist movement soon took off (the word abolitionism itself dates from 1787). By 1804, the various northern states had abolished slavery. On January 1, 1808, there was a nationwide ban on the slave trade from Africa. Along with the United Kingdom, the U.S. established a control on smuggling slaves in 1814.

In the Southern States, slaves worked in sugar cane cultivation and on cotton and tobacco plantations. These supplied the cotton for the English textile industry and some also wished to be able to keep slaves on plantations in the newly reclaimed states. From the end of the 18th century, protests against slavery increased. The Act Prohibiting Importation of Slaves prohibited the importation of new slaves from Africa since 1808. The sale of slaves born in the US was still possible. Slave owners therefore often had to rely on the natural growth of their stock and forced the women to bear children. In 1819, a regulation ensured that states north of 36°30' latitude were no longer allowed to keep slaves. States south of this latitude were still allowed to do so. Beginning in 1830, the magazine Liberator appeared in the U.S. North with propaganda for abolitionism, the goal of abolishing slavery. It got on the nerves of Southerners to such an extent that they hunted down the abolitionists and burned their writings. Northern states were required by federal laws to turn over escaped slaves and allow bounty hunters to track down escaped slaves.

In addition, citizens, with dark skin color, were regularly kidnapped and sold into the slave states. The ideology also blocked all political options; no one wanted to get their fingers on the problem. The British Empire abolished slavery in 1833 after criticism from both religious and economic quarters. For example, Adam Smith argued that a free worker was more productive than a slave and that entrepreneurs with slaves did not innovate. Slavery was no longer prevalent in the North by 1860 because the system no longer proved resistant to the lack of returns.

The North also found slavery increasingly morally objectionable. The Quakers set up the Underground Railroad to help runaways. This secret escape network used code language from railroad jargon. A "conductor" was a helper on the road and a "station" a safe place. Slaves traveled mostly at night and by boat because the chances of being caught were lower on the rivers. Bounty hunters pursued them like bloodhounds along hundreds of miles of escape routes that usually ran northwest to free states. Those who fled north were advised to follow the North Star. The Railroad led to political disagreement and compromise. In 1850, the "Fugitive Slave Law" made helping runaways a criminal offense and it even became mandatory to send them back, even in the Northern states. Nevertheless, the Railroad continued to exist, much to the annoyance of the South.

The underground railroad

The Underground Railroad was a clandestine network of (often ad hoc) smuggling routes in the United States through which escaped slaves could leave the southern states of the United States and seek safe haven in northern states that protected runaway slaves, or else in Canada.

Political Background

The Railroad was a source of great resentment between the North and South of the United States.

Many northerners sympathized with those who helped bring escaped slaves to safety. Southerners demanded for years the enactment of sweeping laws to make the rounding up of runaway slaves mandatory. In 1850, Congress passed such laws. This prevented former slaves from remaining in the United States and eliminated all Railroad routes that did not run to Canada.

(illustration of freed slaves running to Canada)

Operation

The Underground Railroad consisted of hiding places and other facilities owned by sympathizers of the abolitionist movement. It operated like many large-scale resistance movements: with many loose cells that knew little about other cells and really only knew a few of their "neighboring cells." Fleeing slaves traveled from one way station to another, reaching the North in several stages. The main employees of the Railroad were former slaves in addition to Quakers (members of the Society of Friends) and members of the Wesleyan Methodist Church (a Methodist movement of Protestantism), who had a religious aversion to slavery.

The main final destination of runaway slaves on the Railroad was the southern Canadian state of Ontario around the Niagara Peninsula and the town of Windsor. Approximately 30,000 people successfully fled to Canada. This led to a significant population increase in the still sparsely populated Canadian colonies and these settlers formed the basis for the current black population of Ontario.

The Underground Railroad ceased to exist after the outbreak of the American Civil War in 1861.

John Brown's Raid

On October 16, 1859, radical abolitionist John Brown led a raid on the arsenal: he hoped to capture weapons to use to arm slaves in the South and thus spark a rebellion. Marines under the command of Colonel Robert E. Lee helped the local militia overpower Brown and his men. Brown was tried by the state of Virginia for high treason, sentenced to death, and hanged in nearby Charles Town.

The violent abolitionist attack led by John Brown on the national munitions depot at Harpers Ferry in 1859 was condemned by North and South. The attempt to obtain arms for a slave revolt, however, exacerbated the tension between the two sides.

The Civil War

The American Civil War was a disaster for Harpers Ferry: the town changed hands eight times. In 1861, the weapons and machinery of the arsenal were taken away to the South for the benefit of the armament efforts led by Josiah Gorgas.

In September 1862, Thomas "Stonewall" Jackson captured the city in preparation for the invasion of Maryland that would lead to the Battle of Antietam. In taking the city, over 12,000 Northern soldiers surrendered.

After the end of the Civil War, Harpers Ferry was split off from Virginia with the rest of Jefferson County and Berkeley County (under protest) and annexed to West Virginia.

In the next chapters we will further discuss the events of the civil war and the abolition of slavery in the United States.

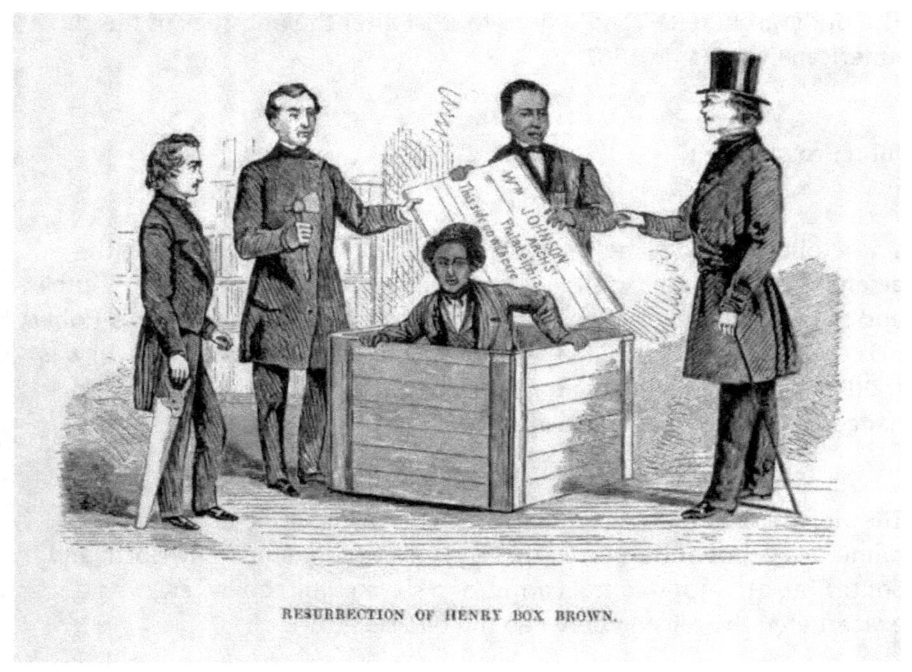

RESURRECTION OF HENRY BOX BROWN.

Chapter 4: John Brown

John Brown born in Torrington, Connecticut, on May 9, 1800, and died in Charles Town, Virginia, on December 2, 1859 was an American militant fighting against slavery in the US. He was hanged in 1859 following a failed attempt to start a slave revolt.

John Brown born in Torrington, Connecticut, on May 9, 1800, and died in Charles Town, Virginia, on December 2, 1859 was an American militant fighting against slavery in the US. He was hanged in 1859 following a failed attempt to start a slave revolt.

Kansas

Brown was born in Connecticut but spent most of his childhood in Ohio. He studied briefly in Massachusetts and Connecticut before returning to Ohio. In 1820 he married Dianthe Lusk with whom he would have 7 children. In 1833, one year after the death of his first wife, he married Mary Ann Day who was 17 years younger than himself. With his second wife, Brown had 13 more children. Starting in 1837, he worked intensively for the abolition of slavery in the United States, including an educational program for young blacks.

In 1855 Brown and some of his sons left for Kansas, where a battle was going on between pro- and anti-slavery factions for control of the territory. This battle (Bleeding Kansas) would be decisive in determining whether Kansas would join the Union as a slave state or a free state. Brown led a group of abolitionists against the group of pro-slavery militants operating out of Missouri. In May 1856, Brown and his group retaliated for the murder of abolitionists in Lawrence, Kansas, by killing 5 militants near Pottawatomie Creek. This act earned Brown national notoriety.

After elections in Kansas finally made the territory slave-free, Brown returned and made plans to start an armed rebellion among slaves in the southern states of the U.S. He was the first person to do so. He raised money, including from Gerrit Smith, to provide arms and ammunition and gathered a group of men around him to carry out his plan.

Harpers Ferry

Brown rented a farm near Harpers Ferry (Virginia, now in West Virginia) with the goal of capturing a U.S. Army weapons depot. With only 21 men, far fewer than Brown had hoped, the group attacked the depot on October 16, 1859, and took the town of Harpers Ferry.

His plan was to distribute the weapons and ammunition in the depot to slaves, and spark an uprising, starting in Virginia. News of the attack reached Washington D.C. the next day after which a unit of Marines commanded by Robert E. Lee along with local militia surrounded Brown and his men. A brief encounter ensued in which ten of Brown's men (including two of his sons) were killed. Seven others, including Brown himself, were captured.

John Brown was then tried and found guilty of treason and sentenced to death. His trial was widely reported by the (northern) media. Brown was variously dismissed as a martyr for black slaves or as America's first terrorist. Frederick Douglass, the well-known black abolitionist, disapproved of his violent methods while others portrayed him as a hero.

On December 2, 1859, Brown was executed by hanging.

Polarization

Brown's militant fight against slavery and his execution further polarized opinions in the country about slavery. Less than two years after his execution, the American Civil War broke out, and Northern Union soldiers sometimes sang the song John Brown's Body written in Brown's honor before going into battle.

Chapter 5: The Civil War

The American Civil War (War Between the States) was a four-year conflict from 1861 to 1865 in the United States between the Northern States (the Union) and the Southern States (the Confederacy). Bloody battles and campaigns took place in many states. The war began with an attack by the Confederacy on Fort Sumter on April 12, 1861. The Battle of Bull Run on July 21, 1861, was the first major battle.

The war was effectively over after the surrender of General Robert E. Lee following the Battle of Appomattox in early April 1865. The last battle was fought on May 13, 1865, at Palmito Ranch in Texas. In June, the South surrendered, and the Northerners won. There were an estimated 695,027 killed and 543,926 wounded.

Causes of the Civil War

Several causes were at the root: political tensions between the federal government and the states; between Republicans and Democrats; economic tensions between the industrial North and the agricultural South or protectionism versus the free trade idea and social tensions due to Southern slavery and large land ownership versus Northern small farmers. There was also a registration law that the Southern states did not agree with.

Uncle Tom's cabin

The idea that the war arose to abolish slavery can be nuanced. This idea originated in part with the reactions to the abolitionist novel The Cabin of Uncle Tom, written by Harriet Beecher Stowe. The 1850 Act inspired her to write about inhumane slavery and the book became a bestseller.

However, the abolition of slavery was a result of the Civil War, not a cause. The conflict initially involved an out-of-control dispute over the extension of slavery to the newly formed states, known as territories. As the U.S. expanded westward, the question arose of whether these states could have slaves. The Northerners felt nothing for the expansion; the Southern Democrats believed that owners of slaves could take their property anywhere.

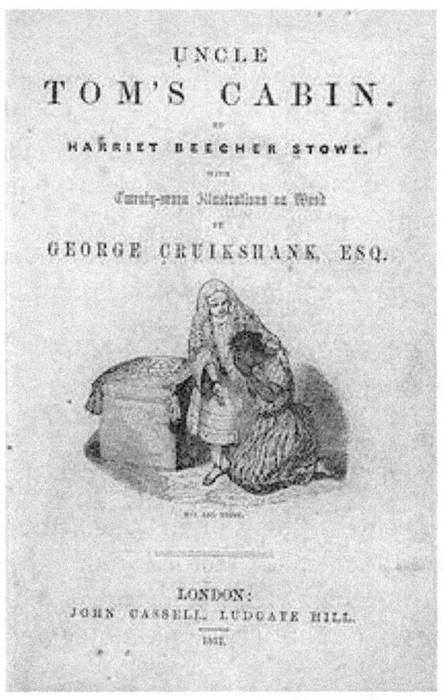

UNCLE
TOM'S CABIN.
HARRIET BEECHER STOWE.
GEORGE CRUIKSHANK, ESQ.
LONDON:
JOHN CASSELL, LUDGATE HILL.

(The book cover of uncle Tom's Cabin)

A military decision

In 1862, Lincoln found in the abolition of slavery a means of preventing foreign interference in the war. England and France had not held slaves for decades and criticized slavery in the U.S. Abolition would make it morally impossible for them to side with the South. To that end, Lincoln signed a presidential order. The Emancipation Proclamation decreed that all slaves from rebellious areas were free.

Lincoln killed two birds with one stone: he was rid of the foreign threat AND he increased the troop strength of his pressurized army by nearly 200,000 motivated black individuals. It was against this background that Lincoln sent a proposal to Congress for the first amendment to the Constitution in nearly seventy years: an amendment abolishing slavery. With this amendment in hand, leaders of the free, black community called on all black people to sign up en masse for military service. Frederick Douglass' efforts in this area are famous.

In early 1864, the first colored companies came under arms, and soon black people were deployed all along the line - to the dismay of Southerners, who did not take black soldiers as prisoners of war after surrender but slaughtered them. Lincoln did saddle himself with another problem by his proclamation. The civilian population of the North feared that the freed slaves would compete in their labor market. In doing so, Lincoln took an unpopular measure during an already unpopular war.

The economy before the Civil War

By 1860, the Southern states felt economically disadvantaged. The North was the industrialized center of the United States. Metal companies, weaving mills, slaughterhouses, gun factories, and other innovative industries brought wealth there. The North operated 110,000 factories with 1.3 million workers; the South had only 18,000 factories with 110,000 workers.

The North owned 32,000 km (22,000 miles) of railroad infrastructure, the South 14,400 km (9,000 miles). In 1860, the North produced 470 steam locomotives, compared to only 17 in the South. The North's conversion to war production was also smoother: the North produced 32 times more arms than the South, accounting for almost 97 percent of the arms industry. The North was also more modern, more democratic, and more liberal. Compared to the North, the South was poorly endowed.

The agrarian economy of the pseudo-aristocratic South was feudal and traditional: some grain and wheat was grown, but the economic heavyweight rested with the wealthy large landowners who cultivated cotton and tobacco with slaves.

The North not only developed more rapidly than the South, but it also distributed its wealth better. Industry brought jobs to the little guy. In the South, the landless could choose between living in marginality or an existence as a servant or soldier.

The imbalance in wealth had been brought about primarily by the unilateral development of the Southern economy and its dependence on food imports from the West, imports of manufactured goods and utensils from the North, and credit from the Northeast. Exports of Southern production passed through New York, which pocketed a portion of the profits.

Demographics, Representation, and Taxation

Demographics affected political participation and the tax burden in the South. More educated people and citizens who were able to move moved north.

There the population grew to 21 million against a Southern population of nine million, including four million slaves. The population of a state determined the number of delegates to Congress. The Senate always had two senators for each state, which kept the balance between the slave states and the free states.

In 1820, the Missouri Compromise came about which stipulated that Missouri joined as a slaveholding state and Maine as a breakaway from Massachusetts as a free state. The compromise of 1787 provided that slaves counted for three-fifths (60%) in determining the number of members for Congress as well as in determining the amount of the tax.

States Rights

Another factor that tested relations was the struggle between the states' sense of independence versus the influence of the federal government. The Southern States desired independence from government and distrusted any form of "government."

Incentive

The occasion was the November 6, 1860, election of the liberal Republican Abraham Lincoln as president. The latter ran a neutral campaign so as not to give offence to supporters or opponents of slavery. His desire to avoid the extension of slavery to the West was unacceptable to the Southern states.

(a photograph of Abraham Lincoln)

In addition, he was elected exclusively with votes from the North, California, and Oregon, so the South perceived the election as an attack. On December 20, the first Southern state, South Carolina seceded. On February 6, 1861, Mississippi, Florida, Alabama, Georgia, Louisiana, and Texas joined together and united into the Confederate States of America with their own constitution and the establishment of their capital at Montgomery, Alabama. On February 9, they elected Jefferson Davis as president.

Nine days later, on February 18, he was officially sworn in. This the North, led by outgoing President James Buchanan, found intolerable. On March 4, Lincoln took the oath of office as the 16th president, and in his inaugural address he rejected secessions. He called on the renegades to restore the bonds of Union and sent aid to Federal Fort Sumter for the port of Charleston.

Escalation

The restoration of Union was refused. To reinforce their refusal, South Carolina considered Fort Sumter an undesirable occupation. South Carolina's militia proceeded to lay siege. On April 12, they fired the first shot at the fort and continued to fire until the surrender. In the following days, Virginia, Arkansas, Tennessee, and North Carolina joined the Confederate States. The following states seceded chronologically.

- South Carolina (December 20, 1860)
- Mississippi (January 9, 1861)
- Florida (January 10, 1861)
- Alabama (January 11, 1861)
- Georgia (January 19, 1861)
- Louisiana (January 26, 1861)
- Texas (February 1, 1861)
- Virginia (April 17, 1861)
- Arkansas (6 May 1861)
- Tennessee (7 May 1861)
- North Carolina (May 21, 1861)

Not all slaveholding states joined the Confederacy. A number of states on the North-South border did not, as tobacco cultivation declined due to soil erosion and slavery declined in importance there. Missouri and Kentucky had two separate governments: one from the Union and one from the Confederacy. West Virginia seceded from Virginia and was formally admitted to the Union as a separate state on June 20, 1863.

There had been anti-Union riots in Maryland, including in the largest city, Baltimore. Lincoln had sent troops from the north and martial law had been declared and most prominent proponents of secession had been arrested, making it impossible for the state to join the Confederacy.

Delaware remained with the Union, but on February 18, 1865, just before the Confederacy surrendered, Delaware voted against the abolition of slavery. It was not until February 12, 1901, that this state ratified the 13th Amendment to the Constitution.

Strengths and weaknesses

Opposing states were 11 states with a population of 9 million (of which 4 million were slaves) and 23 states with a population of 22 million. The North was not only numerically stronger, but it also had the advantages of industry and a fleet that blocked Southern ports. The South had better militaries and counted on English and French support. The French and English governments were in favor of the South, but openly did not take sides, because public opinion was Northern-minded.

England depended for its industry and population on the supply of cotton from the South and grain from the North and remained officially neutral. In private, England supported the South by supplying, manning, and arming the privateer ships Alabama, Florida, Georgia, and Shenandoah. The Northerners were outraged by England's conduct. Lincoln initially lacked good military leaders which caused him to suffer defeat upon defeat for the first two years. It simultaneously explains the long duration of the war.

Secessionism

Secessionism - the movement to secede - was not carried by the entire South.

Sam Houston, the governor who led Texas into the Union, called his state's secession the saddest day of his life. He resigned and left politics. West Tennessee also resisted secession. The farthest Winston County and Northern Virginia counties went. They seceded and in 1863 Northern Virginia counties joined the Union as the state of West Virginia.

Anti-War Sentiment

Over time, anti-war sentiment grew in the North. It began when the Union fared poorly, and deaths piled up without results. Between 1862 and 1864 there were war protests in the Union and calls for the South to go. The fact that there were many people living in the North who were not opposed to slavery and wanted to prevent the release of slaves for fear of their jobs sometimes made matters worse, culminating in the uprisings in New York in the Five Points district. Milder Northerners who sought a peaceful solution were called "Copperheads."

Expectation

The expectation in the North was that a great, bloody battle would end the war in ninety days. That battle became the First Battle of Bull Run, on July 21, 1861. The Northerners, under Major General Irvin McDowell, began energetically against the forces of Southern generals Joseph E. Johnston and P.G.T. Beauregard.

Throughout the morning, the 90-day forecast seemed realistic. By noon, Beauregard lured the Northerners into a trap and took over the initiative. By the end of the day, the Northerners fled toward Washington D.C., and it became clear that the war would be long. The South celebrated the victory by moving the capital to the newly joined state of Virginia, to Richmond, close to the border with the North. There, startled and fearing that even more states would leave the Union, they passed the Crittenden-Johnson Resolution on July 25 that confirmed Lincoln's mantra: the war was about preserving the Union, not ending slavery.

The Anaconda Plan

After the loss at Bull Run, Lincoln switched to planning for a long war. His eye fell on a plan by Major General Winfield Scott: the Anaconda Plan. This involved the encirclement of the South and its closure to the rest of the world. Scott was more realistic than the Southern patriots who spoke of heroic struggles for freedom. Scott knew that the South could not survive without supply lines. His Anaconda plan consisted of conquering the course of the Mississippi and Tennessee rivers, blocking the Southern seaports to take Richmond after weakening. The plan was broadly accepted, and implementation began in early 1862.

Until the surrender of Robert E. Lee in 1865 and the end of the war, this plan remained the guiding principle of everything the North did. Despite the effectiveness of the blockade, the Confederacy with General Josiah Gorgas of Pennsylvania managed to supply its armies with arms and ammunition during the war. To carry out the plan, the United States Army split into a Western Army under General H.W. Halleck and a huge Eastern Army, Army of the Potomac 500,000 men in size.

The Eastern Front until 1863

Command was awarded to General George B. McClellan. He prepared to fight across the Potomac River against Robert E. Lee and his new Army of Northern Virginia and advance toward Richmond.

George B. McClellan's training was outstanding and famous, his command in the field less so. He lingered for months before moving up in the summer of 1862. Then he allowed himself to be tricked by P.G.T. Beauregard, who convinced him with a ruse that his division was huge. It took weeks for McClellan to circumvent and arrive at Richmond. There Lee and his army at full strength awaited him. The Army of the Potomac was spectacularly defeated by Lee. Much of McClellan's force was brought under the command of General John Pope - who suffered a crushing defeat at the Second Battle of Bull Run in August 1862.

Civil War Chronology

1861

- **January 1861:** *South Carolina, Mississippi, Florida, Alabama, Georgia, Louisiana, and Texas withdraw from the Union.*
- **February 1861:** *Southerners establish a government and write a constitution.*
- **April 1861:** *Virginia, Arkansas, North Carolina, and Tennessee leave the Union.*
- **April 12, 1861:** *Attack on Fort Sumter.*
- **July 21, 1861:** *Battle of Bull Run, first battle.*

1862

- **March 1862:** *First encounter between two groups turns into a stalemate.*
- **May-August 1862:** *General George McCellan leads the Unionists in the Peninsula Campaign in Virginia.*
- **September 1862:** *16,000 are killed at the Battle of Antietam; the Union wins.*

1863

- **January 1863:** *Lincoln's Emancipation Proclamation abolishes slavery in the Confederate states. About 180,000 blacks enlist in the Union army.*
- **March 1863:** *The Union establishes conscription for all white men up to age 45. Those who can hire a deputy or pay $300 escape conscription. It leads to conscription riots in New York on July 13.*
- **May 1863:** *At the Battle of Chancellorsville, 30,000 soldiers are killed including legendary General Thomas Jackson. His death was a setback for the Confederacy. After being wounded by one of his own soldiers, General Lee said, "He lost his left arm, I lost my right arm." Then the Unionists crossed the Mississippi and laid siege to the Confederates around Vicksburg. Their surrender gave them control of the river.*
- **July 1863:** *General George Meade is victorious at the Battle of Gettysburg. The battle is considered the greatest battle of this war.*
- **August 21, 1863:** *Massacre at Lawrence (Kansas) by William Quantrill.*
- **November 1863:** *Union victory at the battle of Chattanooga, Tennessee.*
- **November 19, 1863:** *Lincoln delivers a short memorable 266-word speech, the Gettysburg Address at the dedication of the Soldier's National Cemetery at Gettysburg, Pennsylvania.*

1864

- **June 1864:** *Lincoln sends Grant east as commander in chief.*
- **September 1864:** *Sherman takes Atlanta.*

1865

- **April 1865:** *Lee surrenders at Appomattox and signs the official end of the war.*
- **April 14, 1865:** *Southern patriot John Wilkes Booth assassinates Lincoln. Afterward, Andrew Johnson becomes the 17th president.*
- **April 26, 1865:** *Booth is found in a tobacco barn and killed.*

- **May 13, 1865:** *Battle of Palmito Ranch, Texas.*

The so-called "Black Codes" curtail the rights of former slaves in the South.

Battles and Combat Gallery.

The 'Radical Reconstruction' from 1866 to 1873, with Congress voting for the Fourteenth and Fifteenth Amendments, giving ex-slaves civil rights and the right to vote. The 'Military Reconstruction Act' of 1867 divided the South into five districts, governed by a general. The states in these districts absorbed the Union in 1868 and 1870.

The "Redemption" between 1873 and 1877, when the extremely racist Southerners regained control of their South and defeated the Republicans there. After ten years, the Southern States seized on the controversy surrounding the presidential election of Rutherford B. Hayes to get rid of Reconstruction and reverse democratization.

The North-South Relationship

The war had profound effects on America. Even now, southerners feel disadvantaged by the imposed Reconstruction after slave freedom. The prewar contradictions were not resolved but relieved by new variations. The political, economic, and industrial center of gravity of the country remained in the North. The Northern migration of whites and blacks remained. Initially, they migrated to Chicago's slaughterhouses to work in the processing cattle industry in the cowboy era from 1870 to 1900, later they roamed toward Detroit for the automobile industry.

California and New York also attracted people. The Southern States fell into decline or remained stuck in the agrarian economy that continued to unfairly distribute wealth. Plantation owners went bankrupt out of an inability to transition to work without slaves. At the same time, cities fell into decline.

In the North, buildings rose from stone and later steel; in the South, everything was hastily constructed from wood that suffered from the weather because maintenance was unaffordable. Atlanta, which had been destroyed by Sherman, was rebuilt but slipped into a hamlet.

New Orleans retained some grandeur as a port city, Richmond became a mining capital and not the metropolis of before. In Texas, things improved when oil was found there. The rights of the states, so insisted upon by the South, gave way to federal power with the ratification of the Twelfth Amendment in 1865 and with an amendment on the federal income tax in 1916.

The diminished influence was reflected in Congress and the White House - for nearly eighty years all the prominent people came from the North or West. The United States had changed from a confederation of states to a federal state.

Abraham Lincoln

Both publicly and privately, Lincoln let it be known that he thought slavery was immoral, but he also felt there was little that could be done about it without constitutional amendments.

Abolishing slavery was a political issue. Even before the war, Lincoln had stated in a speech that he believed the Union could not remain divided on the slavery issue. The American "divided house" ("House divided") could not remain in place. It would not fall, he argued, but it would cease to be divided and become wholly slaveholding or wholly free.

As far as the Civil War was concerned, Lincoln's goal was to secure the Union and end the Southern rebellion. Abolishing slavery was not a military goal when the war broke out, but only became one after Lincoln, through the Emancipation Proclamation of 1862, declared slaves in rebellious states "forever free."

There were three currents within Lincoln's Republican party:

The radicals, who wanted to emancipate slaves,

The conservatives, who hoped for abolition because they were convinced that blacks were inferior and their presence in America was not desirable. They linked their pursuit of abolition to their return to Africa. The state of Liberia has its origins because of this.

The moderates such as Lincoln who abhorred slavery but feared the consequences of emancipation. Lincoln's view gradually changed in 1862. On March 13, runaways or "contrabands" were prohibited from being returned from a military standpoint. Lincoln's proposal to compensate slave owners in the border states for the release of slaves was rejected on July 12, 1862.

The argument for the abolition of slavery became the seizure of enemy resources out of military necessity. The four million slaves were important to the war effort. We must free the slaves or be ourselves subdued, it sounded.

Unintentionally, Lincoln became an icon of abolitionism. To the freed blacks, he was almost considered a saint.

This was reinforced by his reconstruction plan and the reintegration (Reconstruction) of the South. The fact that he was assassinated (eight months before the ratification of his amendment) contributed to the image of the visionary president.

Chronology of the aftermath of the Civil War

- **1866:** *Congress votes to pass the Civil Rights Act in response to the Black Codes of the South.*
- *Veterans establish the Ku Klux Klan. The South's so-called 'Black Codes' continue to curtail the rights of former slaves .*
- **1867:** *In response to the 'Black Codes,' the government responds with the 'Reconstruction Acts' which places the Southern states under military rule and forces them to grant rights to blacks.*
- **1868:** *The Fourteenth Amendment grants civil rights to slaves.*
- **1870:** *The Fifteenth Amendment gives former slaves the right to vote.*
- **1876:** *The Jim Crow laws reverse the anti-discrimination laws of Reconstruction.*

(An illustration from the reconstruction)

A new type of war

The significance of this war is important not only from the socio-political perspective for its consequences. The Civil War also marks a historical turning point in military-industrial terms because it marks the transition from an agrarian struggle, to an industrial war. In this war, technology changed tactics.

Weapon Construction

Weapon construction improved heat dissipation, reloading, and precision. In 1863, the Union introduced the "Minié bullet." This French bullet type rotated and was therefore more stable and accurate. Manufacturers such as Colt and Winchester designed multi-loaders with up to fifteen cartridges at a time. Confederate soldiers said the Northerners could load on Mondays and keep shooting all week long.

The Gatling gun was a precursor to the machine gun.

The introduction of the train allowed heavy weapons to be transported quickly. Special was the introduction of the Ironclads, the first iron steam battleships.

Although several navies were already experimenting with iron ships, the Americans were the first to use steam engines for propulsion.

Famous is the Union ship the USS Monitor, an armored ship with iron over an oak hull with the very first gun turret. This ship delivered the first battle between two ironclad ships on March 8 and 9, 1862 with the CSS Virginia and narrowly won. This made all the fleets in the world obsolete.

Train and telegraph

The modernization of war did not only take place in direct combat. The context was also changing around the battlefield. To reach the First Battle of Bull Run at the start of the war (1861), men marched to the battlefield and officers came on horseback. Covered wagons, horses, or mules carried guns with difficulty.

Later, Southern rail lines became targets for Northern troops, which slowed and fatigued Southern armies. Their opponents stayed fit thanks to the train that transported rations, weapons, ammunition, and heavy guns. A side effect was that Northern morale remained reasonable toward the end of the war, especially among Grant and Sherman's armies, while Southern morale crumbled after 1863.

Another advantage of the train was that wounded people received better medical care: doctors could get to their direction more easily, wounded people were disposed of more quickly. In addition, the telegraph made remote planning possible. If Grant did something, Lincoln knew about it the next day. In addition to the military reports, journalists reported: for the first time, people knew daily what was happening and who was dying.

War in Cities

Another new development was the arrival of guerrilla militias such as the Southern Bushwhackers and the Northern Jayhawkers, as well as war in the city: although cities had previously been under siege, the Civil War saw the first bombing of cities and fighting. The scale would increase in World War I.

The urban war was a consequence of Grant and Sherman's "total war." Militarily, the North had won, but the South was not giving up. Not only did the opponent's military power have to break, but everything that sustained that power: infrastructure, cities, and the citizenry. In the Civil War, for the first time, civilians were terrorized en masse to force the enemy to surrender. The tactic has since been outlawed by the Geneva Convention.

The white-black relationship

After the Civil War, Congress and the states passed the 13th Amendment to the Constitution abolishing slavery. Although blacks could no longer be forced into labor, they were not allowed to become part of society in the South.

Their daily lives became more difficult than before the war: blacks were not allowed to have contact with whites and were only allowed to work for whites. They were stopped from speaking and voting politically by the poll tax and later, when it became unconstitutional, by the discriminatory "Jim Crow legislation. This system extended racial segregation in the South in which the two "races" lived separately: separately in restaurants and later in buses, different toilets, drinking fountains, elevators, stores, schools, neighborhoods.

This situation lasted until the 1960s, when everything changed amazingly. In that decade, the Civil Rights Movement took off and began an economic rejuvenation and the blossoming of the area driven by the economy of the time. Lyndon B. Johnson became the first Southern president in nearly 100 years. Subsequent change lasted until about 1985.

Although discrimination is a regular occurrence in the South, today the level is comparable to the rest of the country. The Ku Klux Klan is also on the decline in the South. Texas, Virginia, Tennessee, Florida, and Georgia are among the wealthier states; Atlanta is a metropolis and home to Coca-Cola and CNN. As of 1964, there were more Southern presidents than from any other region.

Part 3: Post-slavery society and segregation

Chapter 1: Post-war segregation

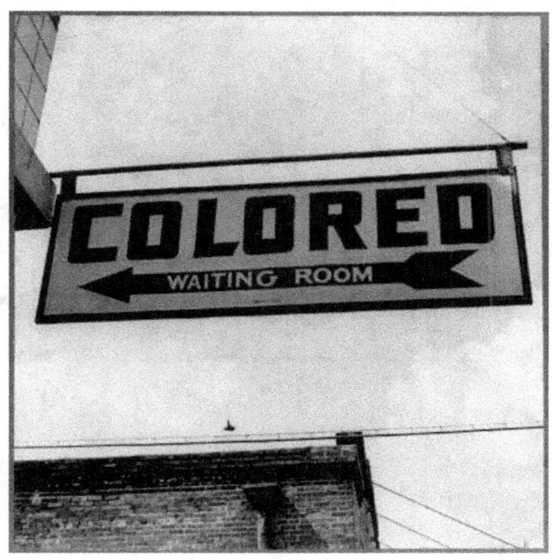

From the American Civil War until the late 1960s, African Americans in the United States were systematically segregated from European Americans. This racial segregation, most pronounced in the former Confederate States of America, existed de facto during slavery, when the states each had their own slave code. After the American Civil War, the Black Codes replaced them, and after Reconstruction, the Jim Crow laws were to perpetuate segregation.

Although these laws went against the prohibition of discrimination in the U.S. Constitution, they held up for a long time because of the separate but equal doctrine. Under this doctrine, things like housing, medical care, education, employment, and transportation were allowed to be segregated by race, as long as they were of the same standard for each race.

In practice, the facilities for African Americans almost always turned out to be worse. Signs were used to indicate what they were allowed to use.

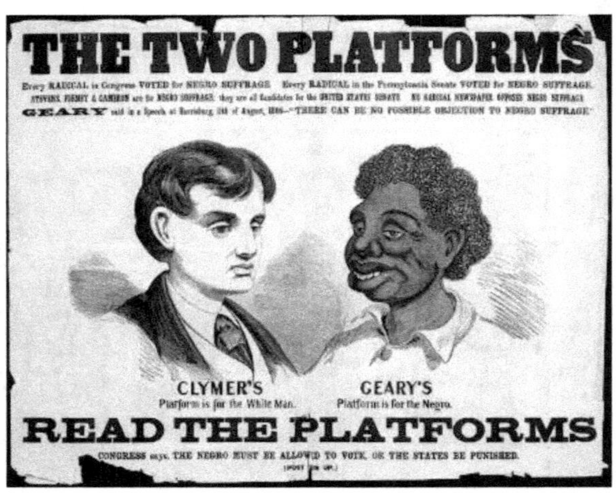

The history of segregation

With the four Reconstruction Acts in 1867 and 1868, the conditions were set for the Southern states to rejoin the Union. One of the conditions was the signing of the Fourteenth Amendment to the United States Constitution. This contained the provision that every person within the territory should be treated as equal before the law. The 1870 Fifteenth Amendment to the United States Constitution prohibited states from depriving citizens of the right to vote based on race, color, and former subjugated status. Under the Republican Party - then the party that opposed slavery - there was a brief liberal and progressive period during Reconstruction.

The carpetbaggers were Republicans who moved south from the north and seized power there. Initially they were supported by southern Republicans or scalawags, but during the 1870s these mostly switched to the southern Democrats. These Redeemers represented the interests of the old plantation aristocracy and used their economic power to wipe out the Republican Party in the south.

This included heavy violence from terror organizations such as the Knights of the White Camelia and the more underground Ku Klux Klan. The White League murdered four members of Marshall H. Twitchell's family, among others, during the 1874 Coushatta Massacre, and the Red Shirts, led by the later Senator Benjamin Tillman, provoked race riots, as in the 1876 Hamburg Massacre.

Lynchings of mostly African Americans also occurred frequently, less than 1 percent of which resulted in convictions after 1900. Historian Joel Williamson called this the period of radical racism. As a senator, Tillman even articulated this willingness to lynch in the U.S. Congress in 1900.

In addition to these atrocities, Jim Crow laws increasingly curtailed the democratic rights of African Americans. In parts of the South where African Americans were the majority, additional requirements for suffrage, such as educational attainment, were imposed. The loss of suffrage also excluded African Americans from jury duty resulting in all-white juries. There was also a ban on mixed marriages in many states.

The compromise of 1877 marked the beginning of the reduction of northern liberal resistance to discrimination. This allowed the Redeemers to increase their influence, while the north lost interest in Reconstruction. The conquest of the Philippines of 1899-1902 under Republican leadership set in motion an American imperialism that Senator Tillman said would result in the Republicans swallowing their criticism of southern segregation. Within the Republican Party, the influence of the black-and-tan faction would thereafter also be diminished by the lily-white movement.

Some 90% of African Americans lived in the South and their loss of suffrage created the Solid South, the loyally Democratic voting Southern states. The U.S. presidential election of 1912 completed this process when Woodrow Wilson became the first Southern president since the Civil War. Under him, racial segregation was also implemented in federal institutions. He began segregating federal jobs at the request of his cabinet in 1913.

Still under the Republicans, a system of public schools had been established in the South that allowed African Americans access to education as well. Integration was not paramount, and thus an informally segregated school system was created. When the Democrats came to power, the budget for this was cut. The Jim Crow laws were perpetuated by the 1896 ruling in Plessy v Ferguson, which established the separate but equal doctrine. In the North, although these laws were not enacted, de facto segregation with separate schools was created. In fact, it would be better for African Americans to receive separate schooling. It was not always the case that laws formalized existing practices. For example, some streetcar companies long resisted segregated transportation.

The hatred in the South toward blacks was such that it shocked South African politician and proponent of segregation Maurice Smethurst Evans. According to Evans, while racial prejudice was justified, he nevertheless found the white hostility toward blacks in the southern American states painful to witness. At the same time, many white southern Americans had a duplicitous attitude, as they depended on their cheap labor despite their great antipathy to African Americans. This was reflected in sundown towns, where black people were not allowed to stay after sunset.

World War I had the effect of creating a pull in the north in addition to the push of Jim Crow laws in the south. Here, because of reduced migration from Europe and increased demand due to the war, the labor shortage in the industrial cities grew, resulting in the great African American migration. A new consciousness grew among the African American population with black soldiers returning from Europe and not being thanked for it, but receiving a hateful reception. In the North, the Harlem Renaissance was accompanied by the stylish New Negro, while Marcus Garvey started the National Association for the Advancement of Colored People (NAACP) and the Back to Africa movement.

In the North, it thus became increasingly clear that the happy darky was a blackface caricature. At the same time, with Garveyism came a more militant stance that advocated its own segregation and thus even joined the Ku Klux Klan, causing distance with activists like W.E.B. Du Bois who sought more integration.

With the arrival in the north, those African Americans regained the right to vote and especially found affiliation with the Democratic Party there. The southern Democrats, however, persisted for a long time in their policy of white superiority.

In the north, however, migration was not smooth either. The arrival of the large numbers of African Americans in the northern and western cities triggered a new segregation, this time an economic one. Of the white city dwellers, a large proportion moved to the suburbs and suburbs, the white flight. In addition, the large supply of cheap labor was seen as a threat by the white working class, mostly recent migrants from backward areas in Europe.

For the South, the disappearance of much of the black population was a dilemma. On the one hand, these had been treated with great hostility, so initially the migration was welcomed. However, as the numbers increased, a problem arose for an economy based on this cheap labor. Thereupon, initiatives were launched to stop the migration. When salary increases and improvements in conditions did not help, attempts were made to impede African Americans' ability to travel.

Senator Narciso Gender Gonzales of South Carolina previously summed up the dilemma as:

Politically speaking there are far too many negroes in South Carolina, but from an industrial standpoint there is room for many more.

After World War II, there was a growing realization that the treatment of African Americans had parallels with German anti-Semitism and that this situation had to be brought into line with proclaimed ideals as a beacon of freedom before true international leadership was possible. For example, the Commission to Study the Organization of Peace (CSOP) wrote:

We may be chastened by Wilson's rejection at Paris of the principle of racial equality-a rejection which embittered the Oriental world. The cancerous Negro situation in our country gives fodder to enemy propaganda and makes our ideals stick like dry bread in the throat. In anti-Semitism we are a mirror of Nazi grimaces.

These motes in our own eye are not to be passed over. There is, however, a vast difference between a governmental policy of persecution, as in Germany, and laggard customs which have not yet been broken on the wheel of a legal policy which forbids them.

We cannot postpone international leadership until our own house is completely in order. Nor can we expect nations to agree that their own houses should be brought into order by the direct intervention of international agencies. We have only to consider the difficulties which any such course would encounter in our own or other countries. Through revulsion against Nazi doctrines, we may, however, hope to speed up the process of bringing our own practices in each nation more in conformity with our professed ideals.

Indeed, the Soviet Union made use of this in response to criticism of human rights violations in the Soviet Union. That criticism was parried from the 1930s onward with references to human rights abuses in the United States with the words *"and you are lynching Negroes."* The Cold War and decolonization made it even more desirable to win the hearts and minds of developing countries in this way.

The U.S. military had always been racially segregated, from its creation during the American Revolution (1765 - 1783) to President Truman's issuance of his Executive Order 9981 after World War II, in 1948.

The last formal forms of racial segregation in the military disappeared at the end of the Korean War (1950 - 1954).

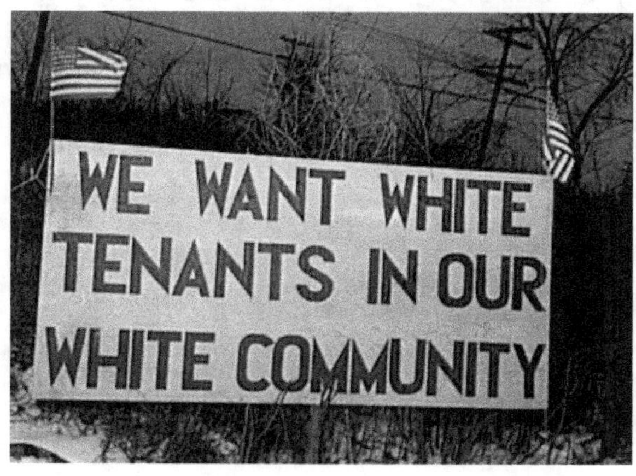

(Sign at the Sojourner Truth Homes, Detroit protesting the black residents in 1942.)

Along with foreign pressure, the African American civil rights movement emerged in the 1950s. With Brown v. Board of Education, although segregation in public schools was abolished in 1954, it would take until 1967 for all Jim Crow laws to be reversed.

On the one hand, the movement consisted of nonviolent protests and civil disobedience such as the Montgomery bus boycott following Rosa Parks' arrest in 1955, the Greensboro sit-ins in 1960, and the 1963 March on Washington. On the other hand, the protest was accompanied by years of race riots, beginning with the Harlem race riots in 1964 and the Watts riots in 1965.

During the long hot summer of 1967, Police Chief Walter E. Headley made the statement when the looting starts, the shooting starts. The assassination of Martin Luther King Jr. in 1968 was followed by the worst riots since the Civil War.

The Civil Rights Act of 1964 abolished segregation in public places, while the Voting Rights Act of 1965 restored the right to vote and Loving v. Virginia of 1967 overturned the bans on mixed marriages. That it took so long was partly because desegregation was associated with communism during the time of McCarthyism, but mostly because of the deep-seated racism among white segregationists and the fear of losing privileges, as personified by Governor George Wallace of Alabama. True integration, therefore, was not complete in 1967, but was just beginning.

Chapter 2: The Ku Klux Klan

The Ku Klux Klan originated in Pulaski, Tennessee in 1865 or 1866 as a local club. According to the writer Wyn Craig Wade, the organization began as a prank by six unemployed soldiers returning from the American Civil War. They dressed up as ghosts on horseback. Soon they began terrorizing the newly freed from slavery black population. In large parts of Tennessee, their example was emulated and chapters of the KKK were formed. President Andrew Johnson pardoned Southern leaders of the defeated former Confederacy beginning in May 1865 after which the Southern states enacted strongly discriminatory laws against black people (Black codes). This virtually reversed the liberation of slaves. The U.S. Congress annulled these laws in December 1865 and decided to proceed with Reconstruction (forced reform) of most Southern states.

Thereupon the KKK quickly grew into a secret organization that opposed this Reconstruction with all its might. At the time the Klan focused mainly on threatening and intimidating the "freed slaves", the so-called Freedmen, so that they would renounce their newly acquired rights.

In 1868, the Klan first gained national prominence when supporters murdered a large number of - black - Republican voters in the run-up to the election. Both the national Klan leadership and the Southern elite distanced themselves from these lynchings. In 1871, the U.S. Congress passed the Civil Rights Act (also known as the Ku Klux Klan Act), after which President Ulysses S. Grant cracked down on the Klan in the South in some areas (North Carolina).

(president Andrew Johnson)

Hundreds of Klansmen were arrested, but due to insufficient capacity, only a small proportion were convicted. By 1875, therefore, this first Klan had been completely disbanded. The U.S. federal government had given up protecting the civil rights of black people, so that in the Southern states black people could be terrorized openly: no secret organization was needed anymore.

It would be almost a hundred years before black people in the South could exercise their right to vote. After Grant, only President Kennedy had a renewed interest in the civil rights of black people.

The first Klan was very well organized locally (but not nationally), as Senate reports during Grant's presidency showed. Because of their structure as a secret invisible group, no data exists on membership. The Klan was, however, extremely popular in the South, especially because of its reputation as the last remnant of the Old South.

William Joseph Simmons founded the second Ku Klux Klan in 1915. This Klan had completely different goals than the old Klan, but used the exact same name and symbols. The Simmons Klan grew rapidly in the 1920s and at its peak had over 5 million members spread across all the states in the South and Midwest. This Klan wanted to maintain the moral hegemony of white Protestantism at all costs and therefore fought all sinners such as black people, Catholics, and Jews. On July 4, 1923, the largest gathering ever of the Ku Klux Klan took place in Malfalfa Park in Kokomo. By 1928, this Klan was also disbanded, although many sections would remain active for a long time.

In the 1930s and 1940s, the remaining Klan chapters chose to massively support the Nazis in Germany and allied themselves with the German American Bund. As a result, the Klan lost its patriotic character and consequently its popularity among the white population.

Only during the segregation crisis in the 1960s did the Klan have a final successful resurrection, but again fell into disrepute due to a variety of bloody attacks and internal scandals.

Today there are dozens of organizations - both in the U.S. and abroad - that pretend to be the heirs of the Ku Klux Klan and have also adopted their symbols. However, their total membership is estimated to be only a few thousand. Most of these new Klan surrogates consist of convinced neo-Nazis.

Emancipation of black people

In the 1950s, a first major problem arose for the Klan, namely the emancipation of their old victims, who suddenly proved capable of fighting back. The black people no longer stood idly by and also began to unite in vigilantes and protection militias.

In 1958, it even came to an armed encounter in North Dakota between the Ku Klux Klan - who organized an overnight meeting - and the native Lumbee population. This brawl went down in history as the Battle of Hayes Pond and caused an identity crisis among the Klansmen.

In 1966, black preacher Stokely Carmichael began a tour of all of Mississippi to address the African American community everywhere. He preached the Black Power doctrine, which later formed the basis of the Black Panther Party movement. He argued that one could only counter white aggression by invariably waiting on the Klan with a gun at the ready. The applications of this doctrine had major implications for the Ku Klux Klan.

In the 1960s, the Ku Klux Klan did find new breath by reforming itself and henceforth focusing on armed aggression against the African American civil rights movement. The most famous examples were the blowing up of a church in Alabama where black civil rights activists were meeting in 1963, the killing of three civil rights activists in Meridian in 1964, and the killing of civil rights activist Viola Liuzzo in 1964. In 1964, Congress passed the Civil Rights Act, bringing a definitive end to segregation in the Southern States.

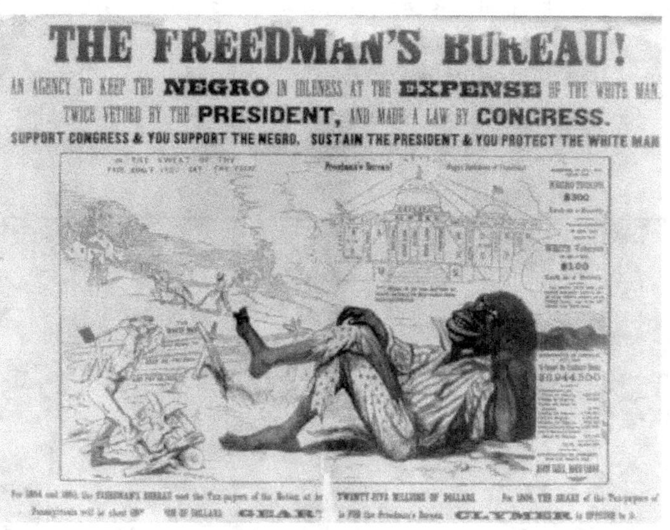

Infiltration and violence

In 1964, the Federal Bureau of Investigation began the COINTELPRO program which consisted of infiltrating the Klan in an attempt to break it up from within. This FBI program involved not only the Ku Klux Klan but also any other individuals and organizations that might disrupt the emancipation process. On the right side of the spectrum this was mainly the KKK, while on the left side it was mainly the Weathermen movement that was targeted.

Even Martin Luther King's peace-loving organization, the Southern Christian Leadership Conference, fell victim to COINTELPRO. Indeed, the program succeeded in uprooting the Klan and increasing internal strife. Within the Klan, everyone was suddenly scorned and suspected as a potential FBI infiltrator, crippling the organization internally. The most famous FBI infiltrator in the Klan was Bill Wilkinson who even managed to make it to Klan leader.

In the 1970s, the Ku Klux Klan faced two new challenges, specifically the phenomenon of practical desegregation and mass immigration. To prevent the desegregation laws from remaining an empty shell, the U.S. government resorted to desegregation busing or forced busing, picking up black children with buses to drop them off at white schools. The Klan carried out several attacks on these buses.

(A march of the KKK)

The most famous attack took place in 1971 in Pontiac, Michigan where ten school buses were blown up simultaneously in a depot. The Klan - under the leadership of the charismatic David Duke - was also actively involved in the South Boston School Busing Crisis in 1974. Then again, especially in California, the Klan organized its own border guards - led by Tom Metzger - against the growing flow of Mexican illegals.

In 1979, the Greensboro Massacre took place in North Carolina in which five members of the Communist Workers Party were shot dead during an anti-Klan demonstration.

During this period, opposition to the KKK also increased. Klansmen's cars were shot at, black children laughed at the masked men. Virtually every Klan meeting was disrupted by actions of armed black militias. Every Klan demonstration was met with counterdemonstrations and violence.

In 1981, Michael Donald was lynched by the Ku Klux Klan. This led to the largest Klan trial ever in which the United Klans of America, one of the Klan's leading splinter groups, was convicted and subsequently bankrupted. This conviction raised doubts within the Klan about its own vulnerability and henceforth made any strict central hierarchy impossible. Especially after the David Duke era, the KKK will break up into small independent Klans.

The Ku Klux Klan in present times

The power and influence of the Ku Klux Klan are still often debated and discussed in the United States. The media also play a very large role in keeping the KKK myth alive - which today would have become a full-blown urban legend - by referring to the Ku Klux Klan at every opportunity.

The trials of Rodney King and Edgar Ray Killen and the assassination of Timothy McVeigh in Oklahoma are just a few examples. Also, the alleged link between the Klan, the John Birch Society and the National Rifle Association contributes to the perpetuation of the Klan legend to the chagrin of both organizations.

There is very little information on the number of members of the current Klans as well as on its finances and actual clout. The official government position is one of silence. A modern Klan does not exist in their eyes. In 2002 the Anti-Defamation League published a report on Extremism in America that said Today, there is no such thing as the Ku Klux Klan. Fragmentation, decentralization, and decline have continued unabated.

Despite this, many researchers still consider the Klans to be the most influential and powerful right-wing extremist organization in the United States and one that is still said to be present just beneath the surface. Especially in the Southern states, the Klan can indeed still count on nostalgic sympathy, but the marginalization of the contemporary Klan by the White Trailer Park Trash and by the skinheads - who have become the prototype Klansmen - does further erode this sympathy.

The last known former Klansman still active in national politics until recently was Robert Byrd, a Democratic senator from West Virginia. Robert Byrd has publicly apologized for his youthful sins and distanced himself from the Klan on numerous occasions. He expressed his deepest regret for his role as Grand Cyclops and Kleagle (a Klansman responsible for recruitment) with the Ku Klux Klan, as well as for his statements from 1958 - when he first participated in the Senate elections - in which he glorified the Klan and minimized or even totally denied all accusations. Byrd died in June 2010.

Chapter 3: Martin Luther King Jr.

King was born as a grandson and son of ministers of the Ebenezer Baptist Church in Atlanta, in the southern state of Georgia. He soon discovered that there was still a lot of prejudice against African Americans in the South and he wanted to change that.

His wish was to make the darker people and the white people equal.

After the death of his grandmother, he attempted suicide at the age of 12 by jumping from the second floor of a house.

At the age of 15, he went to work on a tobacco plantation in Connecticut, further north in the U.S., and was impressed by the good-natured rapport between whites and blacks there. In 1953 he married the musician Coretta Scott.

The 1950's

King studied theology at Crozer Theological Seminary in Chester, Pennsylvania. In 1955 he obtained the doctorate (Ph.D.). He then devoted himself to his ministry as pastor of Dexter Avenue Baptist Church in Montgomery, Alabama, to which his father had confirmed him on October 31 (Reformation Day) 1954. While there, he witnessed an incident that precipitated the civil rights movement.

On December 1, 1955, black Rosa Parks refused to give up her seat on a bus to a white passenger. Black people had to sit in the back of the bus according to local ordinances. The police (also white) were called in and vindicated the white driver and passenger. Rosa Parks was ejected from the bus and subsequently arrested.

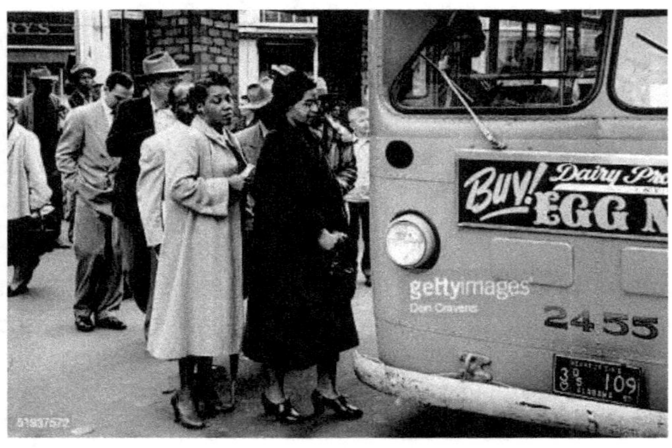

(The Montgomery Bus Boycott)

Montgomery's black community, led by Reverend King, responded to the incident with a successful bus boycott (1955-1956) and achieved a major victory when Montgomery's bus company also had to allow blacks to sit in any seat on the bus. After this, King soon achieved national prominence for his exceptional charisma and personal courage. On numerous occasions he acted as a speaker, denouncing discrimination against black people.

King founded the Southern Christian Leadership Conference (SCLC) and assumed the presidency. The association allowed him to return to Atlanta and dedicate himself to the fight for equality for black Americans, his great example being Mahatma Gandhi, as he too strived for willpower and nonviolence in protests.

King's philosophy of non-violent resistance led to his arrest on numerous occasions. King was hated by supporters of racial segregation in the southern states. There was an attack on his residence and he and other black leaders were convicted on charges of conspiracy.

In 1959 he visited India and, on his way, back he did Lebanon and several cities in the Jordanian-occupied West Bank and the Old City of Jerusalem. He noted back home that there was a border and that if he had visited Israel, he would no longer be able to enter Arab countries. Israel invited him repeatedly in the 1960s.

He took it under advisement only to later cancel anyway. In a letter, he wrote of his desire to visit "the Holy land" (if the agenda of the Civil Rights Movement allowed) and the importance of human brotherhood (Brotherhood), including here. He valued the State of Israel as a democracy. He died less than a year after the Six Day War .

The 1960's

Nevertheless, King's campaigns were successful: on August 28, 1963, he gave a speech at the March on Washington, which was attended by more than 250,000 people and where Mahalia Jackson sang "I've been buked, and I've been scorned" at his request.

In his speech, he described that whites and blacks can live together and spoke the legendary words "I have a dream." In 1964 he was awarded the Nobel Peace Prize. On August 6, 1965, President Lyndon B. Johnson signed the "Voting Rights Act", fulfilling most of King's demands.

King's leadership position within the civil rights movement was challenged in the mid-1960s, when there were voices calling for more militant actions rather than the peaceful protest sought by King.

However, he retained his important position and began to focus on other issues. For example, he criticized the Vietnam War and made his concern about poverty known.

On April 4, 1967, exactly one year before his death, King spoke out clearly against the role of the United States in the war, stating that the United States was in Vietnam to "occupy it as an American colony" and that the United States needed moral changes.

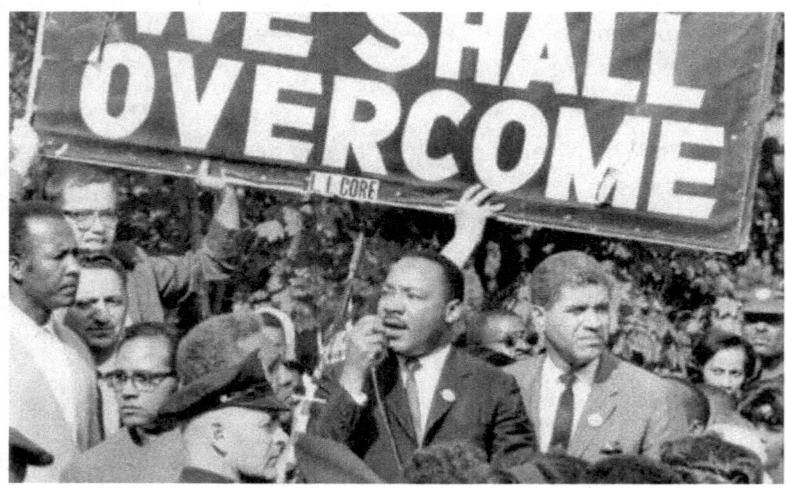

The death of Martin Luther King

On April 4, 1968, King was shot dead in Memphis on the balcony of the Lorraine Motel (since 1991 the National Civil Rights Museum). The assassination led to a wave of riots in more than 60 U.S. cities, killing 39.

President Lyndon B. Johnson declared April 7, 1968, a day of national mourning. King's funeral on April 9, 1968, was attended by over 150,000 people. Millions around the world watched via television. In many countries, the flags on government buildings hung at half-mast.

James Earl Ray, a criminal but one who had not used violence before, confessed to the murder on the advice of his lawyer and thus avoided the death penalty. He was sentenced to 99 years in prison. For the rest of his life, he tried to retract his confession, claiming that there had been a conspiracy. In 1997, this view was supported by members of King's family. Ray died in a prison in 1998. In 1999, King's family won a jury trial in Memphis against Loyd Jowers, who claimed that he had committed the murder for a mob figure. However, many experts were not convinced by the verdict and in 2000, after an 18-month investigation, it was concluded that there was no evidence against Jowers.

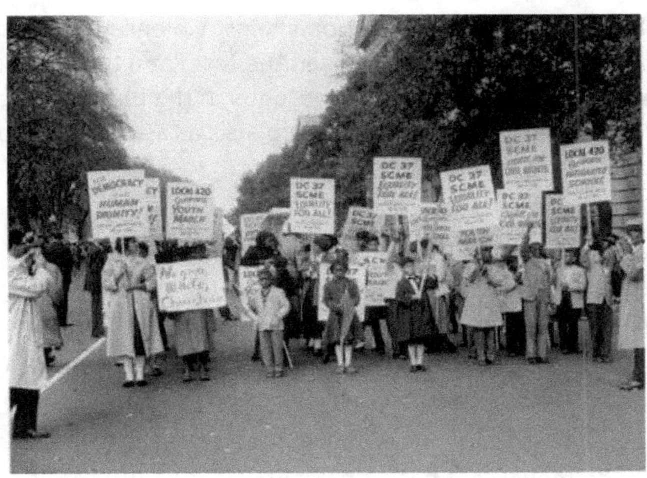

Chapter 4: Black Power

Black Power was a political movement among black Americans in the late 1960s and early 1970s.

Black Power emphasized the expression of a new racial consciousness among blacks in the United States. In a broader sense, the term referred to the conscious choice that black Americans made to promote their collective interests and values, to protect their own well-being, and to gain a degree of autonomy.

The first to use the term "black power" in the political context in public was Robert F. Williams, a writer and publicist of the 1950s and 1960s. The term was adopted by Mukasa Dada (better known as Willie Ricks), the co-director and spokesperson for Student Nonviolent Coordinating Committee (SNCC), a student organization against violence against blacks in the U.S. When Mukasa Dada openly used the term at a time of racial integration, he received support from thousands of the black middle class. This open self-awareness was seen by some blacks as a strategic choice. The term was later used in a milder context.

Worldwide fame came to the Black Power movement at the 1968 Summer Olympics in Mexico City. The two black athletes Tommie Smith and John Carlos balled their gloved fists at the medal ceremony and were subsequently withdrawn from the Summer Olympics by the U.S. Olympic Committee.

Internationally, the movement has a different offshoot. Internationally, the term black power includes African Internationalism, Pan-Africanism, Black Nationalism and just elements of Black Supremacy.

While the movement went its own way internationally, some black activists in the U.S. call themselves "New Africans. They believe that blacks in the U.S. should work for their own independent nation-state made up of the "Black Belt South," where the concentration of the black population is highest.

Chapter 5: Jesse Jackson

Jesse Louis Jackson, Sr. born Jesse Louis Burns in Greenville, South Carolina, on October 8, 1941, is an American Baptist pastor, politician and civil rights activist.

After unfinished studies in theology, Jackson became a close associate of Martin Luther King and was at his side when King was assassinated. Later that year in 1968 he was confirmed a Baptist minister.

Jackson founded PUSH (People United to Serve Humanity) in 1974, an organization intended to involve blacks more in the economy, and in 1986 he became president of the Rainbow Coalition, an organization that brought together various minority groups, peace activists, environmental organizations, and political groups in support of the poor. In 1996, the two were merged.

In the 1980s, Jackson grew to become a key spokesman for the minority and African American civil rights movement in the United States. He attempted twice, in 1984 and 1988, to win the Democratic nomination for president, and although he failed both times, it did show that African Americans had now become a major political factor within the Democratic Party.

Jackson also became known for negotiating, sometimes successfully, with the leaders of countries from other power blocs such as Syria, Iraq, and Cuba for the release of American prisoners, and Bill Clinton honored him with the Presidential Medal of Freedom, the highest civilian award in the United States. Jerry Brown, former governor of California, considered choosing Jackson as his candidate for vice president in 1992. This fell badly with the Jewish community in New York, as Jackson had made several anti-Semitic comments in the past upon which Clinton won the primaries brilliantly.

Jackson was later involved in demonstrations against the Iraq War. His son, Jesse Jackson Jr. was a member of the House of Representatives.

Chapter 6: N.A.A.C.P.

The National Association for the Advancement of Colored People (NAACP) is one of the oldest civil rights movements in the United States and a driving force in the broader African American civil rights movement. The organization was founded in 1909 to benefit African American citizens.

The NAACP's headquarters are in Baltimore, Maryland, but there are also offices in California, New York, Michigan, Missouri, Georgia, and Texas. Each of these regional offices is concerned with the organization's activities in its respective and surrounding states.

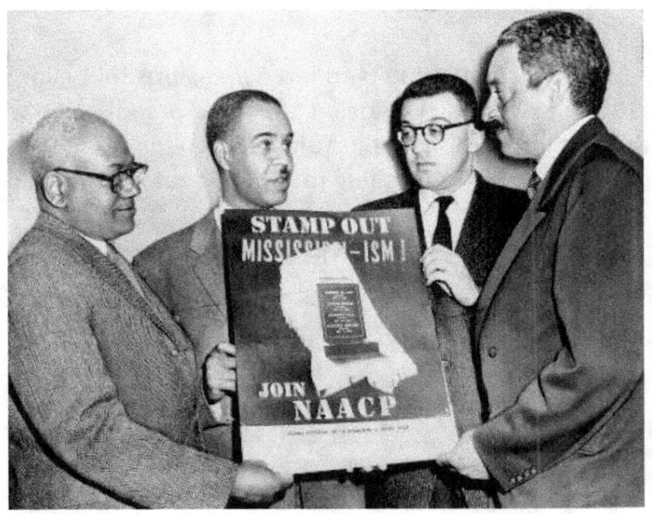

History of the NCAAP

In 1905, 32 prominent African Americans, led by William DuBois, met to discuss the problems of "colored people" and possible solutions to them. Because of the racial segregation in hotels, the 32 met in a hotel on the Canadian side of Niagara Falls; therefore, they were also called the Niagara Movement.

A year later, three whites joined the group: William Walling, a journalist, and social workers Mary White Ovington and Henry Moscowitz. To expand the group's capital and thus its capabilities, sixty prominent Americans were asked to join. A conference was arranged to take place on February 12, 1909 (Abraham Lincoln's 100th birthday); although the meeting did not take place until more than three months later, this date is often cited as the date of founding of the NAACP.

On May 30, 1909, the Niagara Movement met in New York. At this meeting, the National Negro Committee, with forty members, was formed. Among those present was civil rights activist Ida Wells. In 1910, the name of the organization was changed to the National Association for the Advancement of Colored People.

The NAACP primarily used lawsuits to force measures that guaranteed equality between blacks and whites. In 1954, the organization won a lawsuit in the Federal Supreme Court on behalf of black schoolchildren from four different states, abolishing racial segregation in public schools.

Chronology of the NCAAP

1909 - 1941

- **1909:** *On February 12, the National Negro Committee is formed. Among its founders are Ida Wells, William DuBois, and William Walling.*
- **1910:** *The NAACP begins filing lawsuits in the Pink Franklin case to help a black farmhand who had killed a police officer when the latter broke into his home at 3 a.m. to arrest him for trespassing.*
- **1913:** *The NAACP demonstrates against President Woodrow Wilson's decision to officially introduce racial segregation into the federal government.*
- **1914:** *Professor Emeritus Spingarn of Columbia University becomes president of the NAACP, and recruits a number of important Jewish leaders to the organization.*
- **1915:** *The NAACP organizes a national protest against D.W. Griffith's racist silent film Birth of a Nation.*
- **1917:** *In Buchanan v. Warley, the United States Federal Supreme Court rules that states cannot force African American citizens to live in different neighborhoods than whites. Also, the NAACP won a court case allowing blacks to become officers in the military.*
- **1918:** *After the NAACP pressured him, President Wilson declared himself an opponent of lynching.*
- **1919:** *The NAACP sends an envoy to Arkansas, where two hundred black farmers had been murdered in October. The organization provides lawyers for fifty blacks who were tried the next month in a white-dominated trial.*
- **1920:** *The NAACP's annual conference is held in Atlanta, Georgia, to bring the Ku Klux Klan to heel.*
- **1922:** *NAACP ads appear in national newspapers presenting facts about lynching.*
- **1930:** *After protests by the NAACP, candidate John Parker is denied a seat on the Federal Supreme Court because he approved discriminatory laws.*
- **1935:** *Charles Houston and Thurgood Marshall, two lawyers for the NAACP, win a lawsuit requiring the University of Maryland's law school to admit a black student.*

- **1939:** *After the Daughters of the American Revolution ban a black singer from performing at their headquarters, the NAACP moves its concert to the Lincoln Memorial, where it draws 75,000 spectators.*
- **1941:** *During World War II, the NAACP took action to ensure that President Franklin Roosevelt would have a non-discriminatory policy in the war industry.*

1950 - 1990

- **1954:** *The NAACP wins the lawsuit Brown v. Board of Education, making racial segregation in public schools illegal.*
- **1955:** *Civil rights activist and NAACP member Rosa Parks refuses to give up her seat on a bus in Montgomery, Alabama to a fellow white passenger, laying the groundwork for public dislike of segregation in the United States.*
- **1960:** *In Greensboro, North Carolina, youth members of the NAACP hold nonviolent protests in segregated canteens. The demonstrations lead to the desegregation of more than sixty stores.*
- **1963:** *After a mass demonstration for equal rights for blacks, the one advisor to the NAACP, Medgar Evers, is murdered in front of his home in Jackson, Mississippi.*
- **1963:** *The NAACP lobbies for passage of the Equal Employment Opportunity Act.*
- **1964:** *The Federal Supreme Court rules that the state of Alabama may not ban the NAACP's activities.*
- **1965:** *The NAACP welcomes its 80 000th member.*
- **1983:** *More than 850 000 black voters register at the NAACP's urging. Also, the Federal Supreme Court rules in a case brought by the university that President Ronald Reagan may not give tax relief to the segregated Bob Jones University.*
- **1985:** *The NAACP organizes a large anti-apartheid demonstration in New York.*
- **1989:** *Many members of the NAACP walk in a silent march of 100,000 people to demonstrate against Supreme Court decisions that had reversed several earlier rulings against discrimination.*

1990 and beyond

- **1991:** *When Ku Klux Klan leader David Duke made himself available as a senator in Louisiana, the NAACP called on blacks to register. In the end, there was a 76 percent turnout among black voters, so Duke was not elected.*
- **1995:** *The widow of murdered Medgar Evers, Myrlie Evers-Williams, joins the NAACP board.*
- **1996:** *Kweisi Mfume leaves the House of Representatives to become director of the NAACP.*
- **2000:** *Thanks in part to actions by the NAACP, the presidential election has the highest turnout of black voters ever.*
- **2000:** *On January 17, more than fifty thousand people protest an NAACP protest march in Columbia, South Carolina, for equal rights.*

Chapter 8: Harlem Renaissance

The Harlem Renaissance was an intellectual, social, and artistic movement of African American writers and artists that emerged in the 1920s. Often the name is associated with black American writers during that period. In Dutch, the name is therefore used untranslated. Important representatives and founders were Alain Locke and Zora Neale Hurston.

Foreplay of the Harlem Renaissance

The literature about and of blacks had, in the early stages, carried a defensive character. It turned against slavery in some way and was often written by whites. The best-known example, of course, is Uncle Tom's The Negro Cabin by Harriet Beecher Stowe. But blacks themselves also described their plight, sometimes in texts of a higher literary content than Uncle Tom. Such a text often emphasized the fact that the black was also a human being, who moreover knew how to adapt to the white way of life.

The American Civil War (1860-1865) seemed to improve the lot of blacks, but progress remained limited. The majority of them lived in the South, the loser of the conflict, a region that lagged behind economically and culturally after the Civil War.

Improvement

At the beginning of the twentieth century, a number of factors brought about an improvement in the position of blacks. In America itself, whites were becoming interested in their way of life and also in jazz, while in Europe ethnic art had become fashionable. From Jamaica a new self-consciousness among the black population came over. This self-consciousness was manifested in the U.S. in such ways as the founding of the National Association for the Advancement of Colored People (1909) and the Back to Africa movement led by Marcus Garvey.

But perhaps the most important factor was a demographic one: before and after World War I, many blacks migrated from the southern countryside to the cities of the north, initially mainly to work in the war industry or to become soldiers.

What had previously been a rural culture now became a culture of the city. This wave of migration is known as the Great Migration. The Harlem neighborhood of New York City was home to more than 100,000 migrants after World War I, and it was here that the Harlem Renaissance began, consisting of black writers and artists who rejected the nineteenth-century stereotypes associated with subservience to whites. They also called themselves New Negroes.

Literary Revival

This Great Migration brought about a cultural revival among blacks that was accompanied by a growing self-awareness. Those who had served as soldiers abroad had found there that people elsewhere were less dismissive of them than at home. Greater self-awareness was, paradoxically, also stimulated by being so visibly different in a new, still hostile big-city environment. The Great Migration itself was the scene of Jean Toomer's novel Cane (1923), but after that Toomer turned away from the movement and from literature. Langston Hughes' first poems, The Weary Blues, appeared in 1926.

The novels of the Harlem Renaissance can be divided into three groups, according to their attitudes toward the relations between white and black: adaptation, cautious self-assertion, and one's own tradition.

Adaptation

In the novel of adaptation, the black person resembles a white person as much as possible. He has a respectable profession such as doctor or lawyer and even his skin is light in tone. An example is There Is Confusion (1924) by Jesse Fauset, herself a French teacher and later a literary editor and thus an example of the arrived black. Her work, however, deals with the self-hatred that was inherent in living amidst prejudice.

Passing (1929) by Nella Larsen even has the adaptation as its title: passing means to pass over, to adapt. Larsen herself was a light-skinned black - her mother was Danish - and her work features light-skinned or racially mixed women.

Cautious self-assertion

In the novels of cautious self-affirmation, one's own black background is chosen, albeit with limitations and defined by the dominant white culture. The poet and novelist Claude McKay gained great popularity with his Home to Harlem (1928), the story of a black deserter who returns to a Harlem in which a race riot is going on and which is bustling with life. Many of these novels are set in Harlem, but not God Sends Sundays (1931) by the novelist and poet Arna Bontemps, who situates his novel in New Orleans.

Their own tradition

A centrality of one's own black habitat, not as a second chance existence, but as the primary scene of the described, can already be found in the aforementioned Cane. In doing so, Toomer wrote an experimental book that includes poetry and drama in addition to prose. Substance is the experience of being black. The stereotyping of respectable black characters is also emphatically abandoned by one of the most important figures of the Harlem Renaissance, the anthropologist and folklorist Zora Neale Hurston.

Her work has the South as its setting; Jonah's Gourd Vine (1934) was followed by her most important work, Their Eyes Were Watching God (1937). In this novel, the language used, especially through the dialogues in regional language, is very evocative and lyrical. At the center is a woman who succeeds in shaping her own life, without even apologizing for it.

The end of the Harlem Renaissance

Hurston's novels appeared in the 1930s when the Harlem Renaissance had already ceased to exist as a movement. The Great Depression had put an end to it. An alternative view, therefore, is that God Sends Sundays had already been the last book of the period in 1931; however, this does not do sufficient justice to Hurston's position. An entirely different factor that had made the Harlem Renaissance a thing of the past was the arrival of a major new literary talent: with Native Son (1940), Richard Wright struck out in a new direction.

Nevertheless, the Harlem Renaissance had an important after-effect. Langston Hughes continued to publish into the 1960s (he died in 1967), and Zora Neale Hurston's influence on an important author like Toni Morrison is undeniable.

Chapter 9: Malcolm X

Malcolm X, born Malcolm Little, born in Omaha, Nebraska, on May 19, 1925, and died in New York, on February 21, 1965 was one of the American leaders and spokesmen for the Nation of Islam, an African-American Muslim organization that fought for equal rights for black people, among other things. He was a founder of Muslim Mosque, Inc., and the Organization of Afro-American Unity. He was assassinated in early 1965.

During his life, he developed from a petty criminal into one of the most militant black separatist leaders in the U.S. who gained worldwide fame as an advocate of Pan-Africanism. His "last name" X is a reference to the past of African Americans who came to America as slaves. In the process, many were given the same last name as that of their owners. The X indicates the loss of name and identity.

The background of Malcolm X

Malcolm was born on May 19, 1925, in Omaha, Nebraska, the fourth child of a total of seven descendants of Earl and Louise Little. His father, a staunch Baptist pastor and supporter of Marcus Garvey, died in a streetcar accident though there are rumors that he was murdered by white racists.

Eight years later, in 1939, Louise Little was admitted to a mental hospital where she stayed for twenty-six years until Malcolm and his siblings had her released from there.

Malcolm left high school and after spending time in a number of foster homes, he moved to Boston to live with his half-sister. During that time, he found work as a shoeshine boy in a Lindy Hop nightclub. In his autobiography, he relates that he was allowed to shine the shoes of Duke Ellington and other famous black musicians.

After some time, he moved to New York where he became involved in the criminal circuit in the Harlem neighborhood. Drug dealing, gambling, prostitution, and robberies define his days for a time. To avoid being drafted to serve in the U.S. Army during World War II, he pretends to be crazy during the medical examination.

Prison

On January 12, 1946, at the age of 20, Malcolm was sentenced to eight to ten years in prison for burglary, possession of firearms, and theft. On the street he was nicknamed Red because of his red hair color, which he owed to the light complexion of his mother, who in turn had such a light complexion because her father was Scottish. In prison he was nicknamed Satan by his fellow inmates because he constantly cursed.

In 1948, a fellow inmate introduced him to the teachings of the Nation of Islam. The Nation of Islam describes itself as a militant Islamic group that holds that most Africans were Muslims before they were captured and deported to America. They proclaim that all African Americans must convert in order to return to their stolen heritage. The Nation of Islam considers itself a nationalist group that seeks an independent state for blacks within the current United States.

Malcolm studied the teachings of Elijah Muhammad, gaining much knowledge about the Nation of Islam. Ella, his half-sister, arranged for him to be transferred to a prison with a less strict regime in Massachusetts. Here he continued to develop through self-study and began an intense, over time even daily correspondence with Elijah Muhammad who became his mentor.

After his parole on August 7, 1952, Malcolm matched himself with a distinguished and bourgeois image with a tie, glasses, briefcase, and watch.

Nation of Islam

In 1952, after many exchanges of letters from prison, Malcolm met Elijah Muhammad in Chicago. At this time, he replaced his last name with the familiar X, in opposition to his slave name, Little. Later, he would go on to adopt the Muslim name El-Hajj Malik El-Shabazz.

His deep commitment to the organization led him to open several Temples around the country and lead services there as a pastor. Because of his ability to deliver fiery and inspiring speeches, he was soon considered the second-in-command of the Nation of Islam.

In 1958, he married Betty Jean Sanders in Lansing, Michigan. With her he had six daughters: Attilah (1958), Qubilah (1960), Ilyasah (1962), Amiliah (1964) and twins Malaak and Malikah (1965).

Malcolm's message of black segregation inspired the young top boxer Cassius Clay to convert to Islam and join the Black Muslims, as the Nation of Islam was called at the time. Malcolm X became his friend and mentor. This membership was noteworthy because until then the Nation had always opposed on principle the sport of boxing, which was considered haram. Moreover, boxing would once again confirm blacks in the (white) stereotypical prejudice of their stupid, submissive, and violent nature.

Around 1963, tensions arose within the Nation of Islam. Malcolm's popularity, and especially his friendship with Cassius Clay, aroused envy in Elijah Muhammad and other foremen of the organization. In revenge, Elijah gave Muhammad Clay the Islamic honorific name "Muhammad Ali" on condition that he break off all contact with Malcolm.

After Malcolm also made disparaging remarks about the assassination of U.S. President John F. Kennedy ("the chickens are coming to roost"; "what goes around comes around"), Elijah Muhammad imposed a 90-day public speaking ban on him on December 4, 1963. Malcolm ignored this ban and left the Nation of Islam disillusioned on March 8, 1964.

In 1964 Malcolm began work on his autobiography in collaboration with Alex Haley.

Farewell to Nation of Islam

Shocked by persistent (and later confirmed by Muhammad's son Wallace) rumors of Elijah Muhammed's adulterous affairs with six young private secretaries and various death threats made against him by Muhammad, Malcolm X announced on March 8, 1964, that he was stepping away from the Nation of Islam and founding the Muslim Mosque, Inc. During this period, he still remained faithful to the tenets of the Nation of Islam. In April of that year, he delivered his famous Ballot or the Bullet speech. In his view, black violence was still justified as self-defense or in response to violence or injustices committed by whites.

Malcolm came into contact with several Sunni Muslims, who encouraged him to learn about their way of believing. Soon he converted to Sunni Islam, which led to making the Hadj to Mecca in April 1964. Faced with the tens of thousands of pilgrims of all races, ranks, and classes, including quite a few white Muslims, Malcolm X, who henceforth renamed himself Malek El-Shabazz, revised his racist ideas of black superiority. His longstanding struggle to force a voluntary segregation of African Americans from American society in order to return to their continent of origin gave way to a, still radical, advocacy of full American citizenship. Although Saudi Arabia did not abolish slavery until 1962, according to Malcom X, Islam preached racial equality, without distinction of skin color. As a result of this new understanding and marching direction, he sought rapprochement with other black political leaders including Martin Luther King. By debating and collaborating with them, he hoped to sharpen and internationalize the struggle for the American civil rights movement. This resulted in a one-time, brief meeting and handshake between both activist leaders during a press conference following a hearing in the U.S. Senate on March 26, 1964. Malcolm X did continue to advocate so-called black nationalism, a Marxist-inspired socio-economic cooperation among black Americans with the intention of establishing their own separate businesses, without (interference from) white citizens.

Malcolm's death

On February 14, 1965, his home was firebombed. Malcolm and his family survived this attack, for which it was never clear who was responsible.

A week later, on February 21, at Manhattan's Audubon Ballroom, Malcolm had just begun a speech when a ruckus erupted in the audience of 400. As Malcolm's bodyguards tried to calm it down, an African American man came running forward and shot Malcolm in the chest with a rifle. Two other men followed and fired pistols at Malcolm. Onlookers managed to overpower one of the killers.

The three arrestees were members of the Nation of Islam. All three were convicted of murder in March 1966:

- **Talmadge Hayer** *confessed to the murder, was 22 years old at the time of the attack, and lived in Paterson, New Jersey. He was a member of the Nation of Islam and had previously been arrested in 1961 and 1963 for disturbance and stolen-weapons possession, respectively. Hayer was released on April 27, 2010, after 17 pardons.*
- **Norman 3X** *Butler of Muhammad Abd Al-Aziz maintained his innocence. He was released from prison in 1985. And was appointed head of the Nation of Islam's Mosque No. 7 in Harlem by Louis Farrakhan in 1998.*
- **Thomas 15X Johnson**, *who changed his name to Khalil Islam, was released in 1987.*

Initially, Talmadge Hayer refused to reveal who his accomplices were. However, in 1977, in two official testimonies, he declared that Norman 3X Butler and Thomas 15X Johnson were innocent and named Albert Thomas, William Bradley, Leon David and Wilbur McKinley, all former members of a mosque in Newark, New Jersey, as Hayer did.

Some independent investigators with considerable knowledge of the details of the case have accused former Nation of Islam leader Louis Farrakhan of involvement in the murder. Farrakhan himself still denies involvement.

Part 4: Current times and (institutional) racism

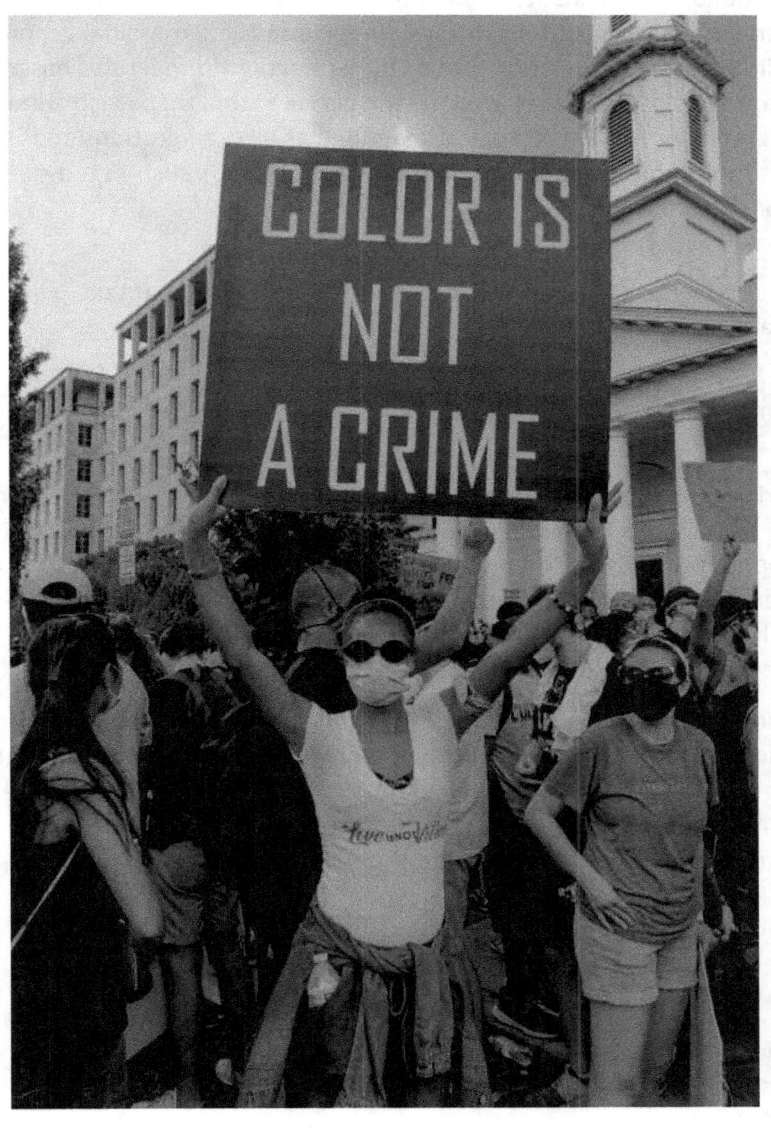

Chapter 1: Institutional racism

Institutional racism, institutionalized racism, structural racism, state racism or systemic racism is the systematic exclusion, marginalization, and discrimination of population groups by formal or informal rules based on institutions. It is irrelevant whether the actors within these institutions act deliberately or not. Institutions are defined as all organizations and structures within society, including abstract concepts such as the rule of law or customs.

Institutional racism differs from other forms of racism that take place primarily between individuals.

History of the term institutional racism

American civil rights activists Stokely Carmichael (later known as Kwame Ture) and Charles Hamilton used the term institutional racism in 1967 in the book Black Power: The Politics of Liberation. The authors were Black Power activists and used the term to describe the consequences of a social structure with a stratified racial hierarchy.

As consequences, they cited discrimination against and inequality for ethnic minorities in housing, income, employment, education, and health. As an example, they cited Birmingham, Alabama, where they said five hundred black babies died each year due to lack of proper nutrition, housing, and medical facilities, and thousands more were physically, emotionally, and intellectually devastated and disfigured by poverty and discrimination in the black community.

They also called institutional racism the confinement of black people in dilapidated housing estates and being daily prey to exploitative landlords, loan sharks and discriminatory real estate agents.

In 1999, British William Macpherson's investigative report into the murder of Stephen Lawrence described the term as, "The collective inability of an organization to provide appropriate and professional service to people because of their color, culture or ethnicity. It can be observed in processes, attitudes and behaviors that amount to discrimination due to unconscious bias, ignorance, thoughtlessness and racist stereotypes that disadvantage certain populations."

Originally, the term was primarily a sociological concept. The concept of institutional racism emerged in the late 1990s after a long hiatus in political discourse. Since then, it has been a controversial concept that is regularly criticized.

The word group has been used in the Dutch media since 1969, peaking in October 2013 when there was significant media coverage of ethnic profiling by police and in 2020 at the demonstrations against racism following the death of American George Floyd.

Definitions of institutional racism

Institutional racism is originally a sociological term defined as follows:

The systematic exclusion and/or discrimination of groups on the basis of written but especially unwritten rules, traditions, behavior, and manners. It is more subtle than overt racism, which is simply recognizable in discriminatory remarks by individuals, and it is unconsciously embedded in the structures of our society.

In the social debate it is usually about unconscious systematic discrimination against certain ethnic groups within large organizations. These can be government organizations such as the Tax Office, municipal agencies, or the police, but also organizations in the business world, such as human resources departments of companies, the hospitality industry, or landlords of homes.

The Cambridge English dictionary defines institutionalized racism as policies, rules, practices, etc., that have become a permanent part of the way an organization or society operates, and that create and help maintain a situation in which, based on their race, some people enjoy structurally unfair advantages and others suffer unfair or harmful treatment. Institutional racism at the state level can also be a top-down, comprehensive system of discrimination, designed to benefit one population group and to lord it over others. This can be done on the basis of ideology, religion, claim to a territory or out of classical racism, where the dominant ethnic group considers itself superior to the other ethnic groups.

Classification of institutional racism

Institutional racism manifests itself in differences in access to goods, services, and opportunities in society. When these differences become an integral part of institutions, they create a common practice that is difficult to correct. Ultimately, this form of racism manifests itself in government agencies, businesses, and universities. One problem with reducing institutionalized racism is that there is no clear perpetrator. When racism is built into the institution, it is expressed as a collective action.

Psychologist James M. Jones, professor at the University of Delaware, distinguishes three ways racism can occur: personal, internalized, and institutionalized.

Personal racism includes actions that stem from racial prejudice, discrimination, stereotyping, disrespect, mistrust, devaluation, and dehumanization.

Internalized racism occurs among members of the ethnic minority themselves and involves the negative perceptions about their own abilities and intrinsic value, such as low self-esteem and low self-esteem of their peers. This form of racism can manifest itself through embracing whiteness, but also through resignation, helplessness, and hopelessness. It can manifest itself in a variety of ways, such as dropping out of school, not voting, or not participating in health screenings.

Institutional racism, according to Jones, is distinguished from other forms of racism by placing racial and ethnic minority groups at a disadvantage to the racial or ethnic majority of the institution through policies, practices, and economic and political structures.

An example of institutional racism is the disparity in the budgets and quality of teachers in public schools in the US. These budgets are often correlated with the value of homes in the area: wealthy neighborhoods are more likely to be whiter, have better teachers, and there is more money for education, even in public schools. Other examples sometimes described as institutional racism include ethnic profiling by security guards and police, the use of stereotypical racial caricatures, the underrepresentation of minorities in the mass media, and finally, the misrepresentation of certain racial groups in the same mass media.

Structural racism

Some sociological researchers distinguish between institutional racism and structural racism. The former refers to the norms and practices within an institution, the latter to the interactions between institutions; interactions that produce different results depending on the ethnicity of the person involved. A key feature of structural racism is that it cannot be reduced to individual prejudice or to the single function of an institution.

Observability of institutional racism

Institutional racism can be deeply hidden in the structures of society, so that people are usually barely aware of it. It may be deeply rooted behaviors. Institutional racism may also be present in regulations, policies, and procedures of an organization.

Institutional racism lurks in homogeneous communities. Members of such a community - consciously or unconsciously - believe that the ideal society should be as uniform as possible. There is then little room for diversity. Minorities and other foreigners are given the task of integrating or assimilating. Members of a homogeneous group also tend to systematically favor members of their own group over those who do not belong to the group in their social interactions.

According to some views, there is a difference in perceptions of institutional racism between female and male victims. Men are more likely to experience institutionalized discrimination, women are more likely to experience interpersonal discrimination.

The consequences

One consequence of institutional racism is discrimination against minorities in the social, economic, and political spheres, which reduces the participation of people from these minority groups in a variety of social activities.

Systemic racism in the housing market creates segregation in black and white neighborhoods.

Fewer job opportunities mean that people from ethnic minorities remain stuck in a lower socio-economic position.

Children from minority groups experience structurally lower expectations in education, influencing their choice of school.

Because of so-called ethnic profiling by the police, there is a greater chance of being arrested, and therefore a greater chance of being caught committing a crime. Therefore, there is a greater chance of punishment.

Lower participation in politics can be a result of institutional racism in the political parties. This in turn can result in less consideration for minorities in the development of laws and regulations.

Institutional racism also affects the self-image of discriminated groups. For example, in the 1940s, the couple Kenneth and Mamie Phipps Clark conducted research with African American children on their preference for the color of drawings and dolls and on their self-awareness. In addition to a preference for a white skin color, they showed avoidance behavior in their rejection of their own skin color. In doing so, they would have internalized cultural preference at an early age.

Housing and mortgages

Institutional racism in the housing sector was seen in the 1930s with the mortgage lenders Home Owners Loan Corporation. To determine the risk of the mortgage, banks relied on the location of the home. In neighborhoods with a high risk of default, the redline neighborhoods, the risk was rated higher.

These were usually African American neighborhoods; while middle-class white Americans could get mortgages, those in those neighborhoods did not. Over the course of several decades, as middle-class white Americans moved out of the inner city to nicer homes in the suburbs, predominantly African American neighborhoods were left behind. Stores also moved to the suburbs to be closer to their (white) customers. From the 1930s through the 1960s, the New Deal and Franklin D. Roosevelt's Federal Housing Administration (FHA) enabled the capital growth of white middle-class people by making loans to banks that in turn financed home ownership by white people, thus enabling the departure of white families from the inner cities.

The banks did not make loans to blacks. Because ethnic minorities were unable to obtain financing and assistance from banks, white Americans gained an increasing advantage over black Americans by making capital gains. As a result, the offspring of the white middle class could be financed from the homeowners' equity when they went to college. This was not possible in black and other minority families.

Between 1934 and 1962, less than 2 percent of government-subsidized housing went to non-white people. The institutional racism of the FHA model was tempered in the 1970s. President Obama's efforts also improved the situation with the introduction of Fair Housing Finance.

The programs described above and funded by the U.S. government have had a significant impact on inner cities. Black neighborhoods are turning into food deserts, but had many liquor stores. Low-income neighborhoods had only small independent grocery stores that typically had to charge higher prices. Poor consumers from these neighborhoods either had to do their shopping in higher-income neighborhoods or spend more in their own neighborhoods.

Today's racial segregation and wealth disparities among Americans of different skin colors are the result of yet other policies of the past. For example, farmworkers and white-collar workers, most of whom were black, were not entitled to benefits under the Social Security Act of 1935. Indeed, landowners from the South did not want government assistance to change the agricultural system. The Wagner Act of 1935 also prohibited blacks by law from joining any union that could provide protection.

Research in large cities such as Los Angeles and Baltimore shows that ethnic minority communities have less access to parks and other green space. Parks have social, economic and health benefits. Public spaces allow for social interaction, enable daily physical activity, and improve mental health. Minority communities also have less access to decision-making processes that determine the distribution of parks.

Systemic racism in health care

Institutional racism affects health care accessibility within non-white minority communities. Ethnic minority groups are more likely to be uninsured than the white majority, which reduces their access to a variety of health services.

This creates health disparities among ethnic groups. Consequently, several diseases in the U.S., including AIDS, are more common among ethnic minorities. In a 1992 article, Janis Hutchinson argues that the federal government has also been slow to respond to the AIDS epidemic in minority communities and that the government has not taken ethnic diversity into account in AIDS prevention and treatment. The relatively high proportion of black prisoners also led to more AIDS infections. These men experienced rape and drug addiction in prison that involved the use of contaminated needles. Because of the large number of prisoners from the black community, their wives sought more sexual contact outside of prison, resulting in higher risk of HIV infection.

Systemic racism in the environment

Institutional racism can also affect minority health through environmental factors. For example, racial segregation disproportionately exposed black communities to chemicals such as lead-based paint, diesel fumes, crowds, litter, and noise.

Systemic racism in the police and criminal justice system

Racism within the U.S. police force is seen as structural by some, but by no means by all. In each case, racism within the American police culminates in murder by police officers. Examples of these killings include those of Michael Brown in 2014 and George Floyd in 2020. A Stanford University study found that African Americans were 20% more likely to be checked at a traffic stop. In Los Angeles, 28% of people stopped by police officers were black, even though they make up only 9% of the population.

Institutional racism also occurs in the criminal justice system. African Americans are more likely to be convicted of criminal offenses than whites or people of Hispanic background. An example of this is convictions for possession of cocaine. Although approximately 2/3 of cocaine users in the U.S. are white or Hispanic, in 1994 84.5% of defendants convicted of cocaine possession were black, while 10.3% were white and 5.2% were Hispanic. Another manifestation of this is that homicide cases with white victims were more likely to result in a death sentence than those with black victims.

Systemic racism in government service

In theory, public servants are appointed on merit. In practice, however, there are reasons that impede the integration of ethnic minorities. The U.S. Department of Labor began enforcing racial quotas in the 1970s, but lawsuits proved necessary to achieve effective implementation of these quotas. In 1971, the Vulcan Blazers of the Baltimore Fire Department filed a landmark lawsuit that resulted in the appointment of blacks to leadership positions in the fire department. Other minority groups followed their lead and went to court as well. In 2009, the city of Baltimore paid $4.6 million to resolve a police officer discrimination case.

Systemic racism in education

Standardized tests are also considered a form of institutional racism, as it appears that these tests favor people from a certain socio-cultural background. However, the causes of the differences in test results are not yet fully known.

It was not until the 1960s that it became possible for young people of color to study at colleges and universities. This became possible through the Civil Rights and Higher Education Acts. However, barriers to integration remained in the predominantly white institutions of higher education. It was also difficult for many black students to attend college due to the poor quality of primary and secondary education in segregated schools.

Systemic racism in politics

Black representation in the U.S. Congress has always remained low since the abolition of slavery. During the Nixon administration, there were 11 black representatives, ten in the House of Representatives and one in the Senate. After that, the representation of blacks began to increase.

Chapter 2: Black Lives Matter

Black Lives Matter (abbreviated as BLM) is an international movement that originated in the African American community in the United States in response to police violence against African Americans. The movement began with the hashtag "#BlackLivesMatter" after George Zimmerman was acquitted in 2013 for the death of Trayvon Martin on February 26, 2012, in Sanford, Florida, an African-American youth aged 17.

Since then, Black Lives Matter political activists have been pushing back against all forms of violence against black people, including police brutality, ethnic profiling, and over-punishment of black people in the U.S. justice system.

The movement organizes demonstrations and protests, and since 2015 has also challenged politicians to speak out against violence against African Americans. Black Lives Matter gained national prominence in 2014 through protests following the death of Eric Garner on July 17, 2014, in New York and the death of Michael Brown on August 9, 2014 in Ferguson, Missouri. Since the protests in Ferguson, many protests followed across the country. Following the death of George Floyd in Minneapolis on May 25, 2020, Black Lives Matter's following grew rapidly internationally, and many protests again took place.

Previous protest movements

The origins of the Black Lives Matter movement lie in the African American civil rights movement. The civil rights movement fought for decades to end racial segregation (racial separation) and discrimination in the United States.

The Black Lives Matter movement states that it further draws inspiration from the Black Power movement, among others. Several media outlets referred to the Black Lives Matter movement as a new civil rights movement.

Online protests

The Black Lives Matter movement emerged in the summer of 2013 following the acquittal of George Zimmerman for the murder of black teenager Trayvon Martin. The movement with the hashtag "#BlackLivesMatter" was founded by three black American women Alicia Garza, Patrisse Cullors and Opal Tometi.

Alicia Garza posted a Facebook message, titled "a love letter to black people," in which she described, "Our Lives Matter, Black Lives Matter. To this, Patrisse Cullors responded with "#BlackLivesMatter. They were supported by Opal Tometi.

Demonstrations

The movement organized the first national 'Freedom Ride' demonstration in Ferguson in the US state of Missouri in August 2014. The trigger for this demonstration was the death of Michael Brown, a black teenager. By police officer Darren Wilson, Michael Brown was shot dead. The officer had fired twelve bullets. Michael Brown was unarmed. The day after this shooting, protests broke out in Ferguson.

Alicia Garza along with the other two co-founders of Black Lives Matter, Patrisse Cullors and Opal Tometi, organized this "Freedom Ride" to Ferguson. More than 500 people from 18 different cities across the United States signed up.

Structure

Black Lives Matter is a decentralized organization. The founders oppose a top-down structure that previous civil rights movements used. Johnetta Elzie, a well-known Black Lives Matter activist, emphasizes that the organization has always maintained that it is made up of many.

According to her, there cannot be one person the leader of the movement, but everyone is a leader. For those who choose to become involved in the Black Lives Matter movement, the movement has thirteen guiding principles that are important such as diversity, empathy, and restorative justice, among others.

Chapter 3: The death of Trayvon Martin

The death of Trayvon Martin occurred on the evening of February 26, 2012, in Sanford, Florida, when 28-year-old Latino vigilante George Zimmerman shot and killed 17-year-old African-American Trayvon Martin (born February 7, 1995 in Miami Gardens). Zimmerman gave self-defense as the reason.

This death and the circumstances under which it occurred led to a nationwide discussion of racism in the United States, which also picked up in other countries. Zimmerman was charged with manslaughter. The trial began on June 10, 2013, in Sanford. On July 13, 2013, after sixteen hours of deliberation by a six-member jury, Zimmerman was found innocent and acquitted.

Zimmerman testified that Trayvon Martin, who was walking through a Sanford neighborhood wearing a hoodie, was acting suspiciously. When he spoke to the boy, a scuffle ensued in which Zimmerman shot and killed the unarmed Martin. Zimmerman claimed that it was a case of emergency defense. Under Florida law, it was permissible to kill someone in emergency defense. As a result, the jury felt compelled to acquit. If the jury had found him guilty, Zimmerman could have received a life sentence. An anonymous juror revealed shortly thereafter that she was convinced that Zimmerman was indeed guilty of the teenager's death. She pointed out the legislation, made it necessary to declare Zimmerman innocent. The juror therefore cried for a tightening of the self-defense law.

Following the acquittal, thousands of people, particularly African Americans, took to the streets in protest, with skirmishes with police occurring. Reverend Raphael Warnock declared that Martin had been killed because, as a black boy, he was not seen as a human being, but as a problem. President Obama, who said that if he had a son who would look like Martin, called on the protesters to respect justice.

Chapter 4: The death of George Floyd

The death of George Floyd, an African American man, occurred in Minneapolis, Minnesota, on May 25, 2020. The 46-year-old Floyd died after police officer Derek Chauvin leaned on Floyd's neck with his knee for more than eight minutes as he lay handcuffed to his stomach in the street. Two other officers simultaneously leaned their knees on his back and a fourth officer kept the public at bay. After Floyd passed out after about six minutes, Chauvin kept his knee on Floyd's neck for nearly three more minutes. Floyd was then transported to the hospital in an ambulance; an attempt at resuscitation in the ambulance was unsuccessful. He was pronounced dead on arrival at the hospital. Chauvin was found guilty of the murder of George Floyd by a jury on April 20, 2021.

The assault was filmed by bystanders with a cell phone and broadcast live on Facebook Live. This caught the attention of the American media. The event became world news and led to protests in Minneapolis and other cities worldwide against racism. Some of these protests degenerated into riots and looting. For some time, U.S. human rights organizations had been complaining about what they saw as discriminatory treatment of blacks by the police, with no improvement.

Four officers were involved in Floyd's arrest. All were fired shortly after Floyd's death. Chauvin was arrested on May 29, 2020, on suspicion of manslaughter, later aggravated to manslaughter. The three other agents were arrested on June 3, 2020, on suspicion of aiding and abetting manslaughter.

Who is George Floyd

George Floyd, father of two daughters and a son, was an American man of African American descent. He worked as a security guard for a Minneapolis restaurant for five years before losing his job due to the corona pandemic that broke out in 2020.

On June 9, he was buried in Pearland, Texas, the state where he grew up. There was a memorial service at the Houston church beforehand.

Agents

Chauvin was a then 44-year-old white man who had worked as a police officer for the Minneapolis Police Department since 2001. He had eighteen complaints to his name, two of which resulted in an official reprimand.

One of three other officers was charged in 2017 with using excessive force while performing his duties. The case was settled out of court with US$25,000. The other two officers had only been on duty for a short time.

All four officers were fired and charged shortly after Floyd's death. The officer who put his knee on Floyd's neck risks a prison sentence of up to 40 years.

Statements from police and ambulance personnel

Shortly after 8 p.m. on May 25, Memorial Day, Minneapolis police responded to a report of payment with counterfeit money on Chicago Avenue South in the Powder horn neighborhood. According to a co-owner of a nearby food store, an employee determined that Floyd had attempted to pay with a counterfeit $20 bill. At this the police were called, who found Floyd in a car nearby. According to them, Floyd had been under the influence. A police spokesman stated that the officers had ordered him to exit the vehicle, after which he allegedly physically resisted. The two officers then asked him to get into the police car, after which he shouted that he was claustrophobic, and he panicked. After this, two more officers arrived for backup, including the officer who kept his knee on Floyd's neck for minutes.

According to Minneapolis police, the officers were able to put the suspect in handcuffs and determined that he was suffering from medical problems. At this they called an ambulance. According to the police statement, no weapons were used in the arrest. According to the Minneapolis Fire Department, ambulance personnel transported the man from the scene and attempted to resuscitate him. They determined that he had no heartbeat and was unresponsive to the medical procedures. Floyd was then taken to Hennepin County Medical Center, where he was pronounced dead.

Live video

Part of the arrest was filmed by a bystander and broadcast live on Facebook Live. This video quickly went viral. In the video, an officer can be seen pressing down on Floyd's neck with a knee.

At the time the video begins, Floyd is already lying on the street with his chest pressed down, while the officer kneels on his neck and addresses him in a humiliating manner. Floyd asks for the knee to be removed from his neck and indicates that he is choking. The officer responds sarcastically with "You can speak, so you can breathe." A bystander calls out to the officer to give Floyd breathing room. Despite Floyd's continued pleas and the bystanders' reactions, the policeman does not remove his knee from Floyd's neck. Floyd finally stops trying to get up, gets a nosebleed. Later, he loses consciousness. The officers ignore requests from bystanders to take Floyd's pulse.

The officer only removed his knee from Floyd's neck when emergency medical services arrived to lift his body onto a stretcher. He was wheeled away in an ambulance. This video shows the police officer kneeling on Floyd's neck for at least seven minutes.

Another video footage

A second video from a bystander, shot from a vehicle, shows Floyd being removed from his car. This footage does not show, according to several media outlets, that Floyd resisted.

A six-minute video from a surveillance camera at a nearby restaurant was later distributed by the news media. This shows two officers removing a man from a vehicle. The man is handcuffed and taken to the sidewalk, where he sits down. A third officer arrives. Later, an officer helps the man get back up, and two officers take the man to a police vehicle, where the man falls to the ground. Although police initially claimed that Floyd had physically resisted arrest, this surveillance video shows officers calmly holding him down. Other video footage supports these described images.

The cause of Death

The initial autopsy was ordered by authorities and initially the result was that Floyd died from a combination of atheromasias of the heart, hypertension, fentanyl poisoning and recent use of methamphetamine. Floyd's family did not trust this result and therefore had a second autopsy performed by an independent party, Michael Baden and Allecia Wilson, and they concluded that asphyxiation was the cause of death. After this second autopsy, the pathologist from the first autopsy revised his report and confirmed "that Floyd died because there was not enough blood flowing to his brain as a result of the neck clamp while he was restrained by Minneapolis police officers.

Floyd's death prompted several days of demonstrations against police brutality around the world

Our Books

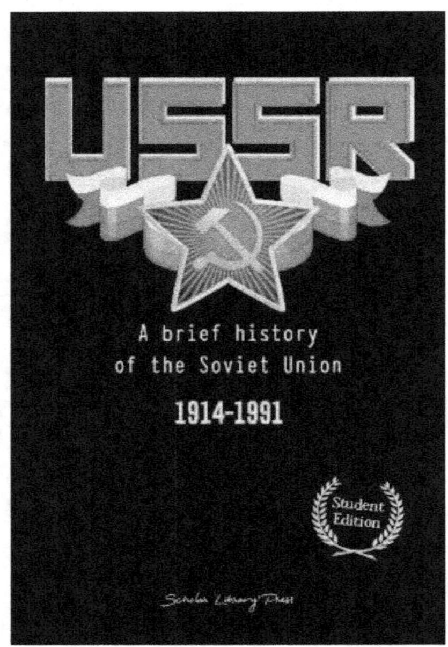

Interested in the history of the USSR?

The History of the USSR 1914-1991 is a comprehensive and authoritative account of one of the most important periods in modern world history. It traces events from Tsarist Russia, through to Lenin's Bolshevik Revolution, Stalin's rule, Khrushchev's "Thaw" and Brezhnev's stagnation - up to Gorbachev and beyond. This book offers an unrivalled perspective on Soviet society at every level - political, economic, social and cultural.

This book is a comprehensive account of the rise and fall of communism in Russia. The author examines how these leaders dealt with economic problems such as food shortages and unemployment. He also explores their foreign policies during World War II and afterward, when they tried to maintain an empire that was slipping out of their grasp.

You'll find out how people lived under communism; what they ate; where they went for entertainment; how their clothes were made; who was allowed to travel abroad or buy foreign goods; what happened when they fell ill or died. And you'll learn about all those things that are now so familiar, but which had not yet been invented then – mobile phones, computers, western movies... All these things have come into being since 1991 but this book will tell you what life was like before them.

You will be able to understand why this country fell apart so quickly after its inception by reading this book! There are plenty of lessons learned for those who want to study communist countries or just learn more about Russian history!

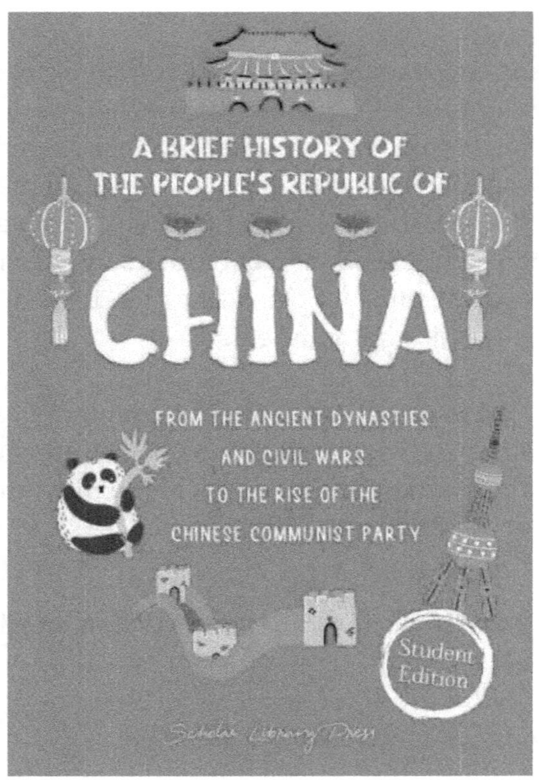

If you are interested in the history of China, this is a great book for you!

This book is a brief history of the People's Republic of China. It covers everything from Ancient Dynasties and Civil Wars to the Rise of the Chinese Communist Party. You can read about how it all started, what happened during Mao Zedong's rule, and more!

In 1949, the Chinese Communist Party (CCP) won its first victory and established the People's Republic of China. The CCP was led by Mao Zedong and his comrades-in-arms such as Zhou Enlai, Zhu De, Chen Yun and Deng Xiaoping. They led the people to fight against Japanese invaders and their domestic enemies including landlords, rich peasants, counterrevolutionaries, and bad elements who were sabotaging national reconstruction.

If you're interested in learning about this country's past, then this is a great place to start. The author has created an informative book that will give you a better understanding on what took place over time. It also includes pictures for visual learners who want to see images as well as words.

This book will tell you about how these leaders helped shape modern day China with their leadership skills that are still used today! You will learn about how they fought for equality among all classes in society while also building up an economy that could compete on a global scale. It is not just a story about politics or economics - it's also one of culture! Learn more about traditional customs from this brief history of China!

You can find this book in a paperback version on all major book store websites

www.ingramcontent.com/pod-product-compliance
Lightning Source LLC
Chambersburg PA
CBHW071750150726
47998CB00005B/1877

* 9 7 8 9 4 9 2 9 1 6 9 1 4 *